Getting Black Folks
TO SELL

George Subira
BA, M.Ed., Ed.S.

Published by

Very Serious Business Enterprises
P.O. Box 356
Newark, New Jersey 07101
(609) 641-0776

This Material - GETTING BLACK FOLKS TO SELL - can
be presented in half day, full day or weekend workshops:

Other Business or Motivational Presentations
are Available as well

For Further Information Contact:

George Subira
Very Serious Business Enterprises
P.O. Bo 356
Newark, N.J. 07101
(609) 641-0776

An Audio Tape Cassette Program

covering the major points in *GETTING BLACK FOLKS
TO SELL* will be available for purchase in the Spring of
1988. The video tape version of this material should be
available in the Fall of 1988.

For further Information write to:

George Subira
Very Serious Business Enterprises
P.O. Bo 356
Newark, N.J. 07101
(609) 641-0776

© 1988 by George Subira

ISBN# 0-9605304-2-8

ACKNOWLEDGMENTS

This book represents a rather significant breakthrough for me in a couple of ways. It was in the writing of this book that I was forced to finally deal with computers, computer programs and "computer talk." Praises are due to the entire staff at ComputerCroft of Northfield, New Jersey. I am particularly grateful to Sherry Branks, the owner, and Melanie Koenig for their efforts in going through the manuscript until this final product was produced.

The second breakthrough came in the person of Debóra Young of The Debóra Group, Stamford, Connecticut. Ms. Young is the first real editor that I've ever worked with. It was amazing for me to watch her go through *my material, change it* and admit that she was right about ninety percent of the time. Thank you Debóra for hundreds of pages and a thousand corrections. Thanks also goes out to my brother Len Trower who gave of his valuable time to help make his brother's book more understandable by the general public.

In doing the research for this book, dozens of books and articles where consulted. But in all honesty, I think two of the books where much more enlightening than all the rest put together. If you are serious about learning to sell read <u>Secrets of Closing The Sale</u> by Zig Ziglar and <u>Unlimited Power</u> by Tony Robbins. Both books are available now in paperback at major bookstores. Finally, I wish to thank Michelle Gluckow of Bookmart Press and the staff there for always coming through with the final, physical products on time, all the time.

DEDICATIONS

This Volume is dedicated to several Black Americans who have had a tremendous impact in involving African-Americans in the Sales field.

To the Late Madame C.J. Walker of Indianapolis, Indian
> Black History records her as the first Black American to earn a million dollars. She did it by building sales organizations in the early 1900's that sold hair care products to Black Women.

To Mr. S.B. Fuller of Chicago, Illinois
> Thank you for turning out generations of Black salespeople. Your legacy will continue for generations to come.

To George and Ruth Halsey of Greensboro, North Carolina
> You two have probably involved more Black people in the selling process than any other two people in the history of the United States (and maybe the World). Thank you for your enthusasm, your dedication and your example.

To Ms. Ruell Cone of Atlanta, Georgia
> Thousands of Black Women have profited from your example. Thank you for your consistency, your caring and your sharing.

Finally to Mr. Dick Gregory of the State of Massachusetts
> As The First Black celebrity to encourage our people in the area of sales, you have impacted tens of thousands of Black folks. People who formerly looked down their noses at selling have now looked up and seen the light. Thank you for this major contribution.

TABLE OF CONTENTS

Introduction

The book you hold in your hands right now is probably the only significant attempt in this century to discuss in some detail the art of selling within the context of the African-American experience. If this is so, then it could very well be that this book is the first of its kind in America, period! Usually a person is very proud of being "a first" in any venture. I wish I could feel such pride, but I do not. I really feel this topic should have been addressed long before now. What I have done in this book is not reveal a "discovery" or "break through" but simply report plain facts that any truly observant Black American could have done just as easily. Because the ideas discussed in this book are so obvious (and so significant in Black Folk's survival in America), it *scares* me that no one has seen fit to report them. As a people, we face specific dangers and opportunities. We must learn to respond to each of them in a proper way. This, in my opinion, is what leaders are supposed to do and it frustrates me when I don't see it being done. I feel a sense of shame that so many people in our community carry the title, officially or unofficially, of leader when in fact they don't know any more about what is going on than the next person. This is both shameful and scary.

The Black media in particular is partly to blame. Out of twenty-eight million equally-important Black Americans, they insist on giving us detailed accounts of the lives of about one hundred. We are notified weekly of the ways actors, actresses, athletes and singers diet and exercise, treat their spouses and children, and generally play out their privileged roles as if this information will save Black America. If the lack of information sharing is so prevalent among the "leadership class" is there any wonder why the masses of our people are so confused. Can you see why they turn off and tune out.

A Time to Reprogram

This book is a tool to try to change your way of thinking. If you feel very secure and comfortable, maybe you shouldn't be. And if you feel lost, helpless or out of control of your life, maybe you don't have to feel that way either. In this volume I will talk about *selling and survival,* because more and more of our people will make it based on their decision to sell or not. This volume is also about *selling and prosperity* because these two concepts are intimately linked. So whether you are looking to just get by and keep your head above water or whether you are looking for financial independence, this book will interest you.

Essentially the task at hand is to reprogram your thinking so that you might find the value and the liberation in selling, if you have not seen it already. This effort to give you a positive view of sales is likely to clash with a lifetime of negative ideas, feelings and even experiences that you most likely have had regarding selling. This is what I mean by reprogramming. I will show how, if you study the things the Black community complains about, many of our complaints can be addressed by more active involvement and success in selling. I will show how "salaries" will never allow Black America to have its fair share of the economic pie, but, how sales success could very well help us meet that goal. I hope to clear up common myths about selling and show the relationship of selling to many other important aspects of our lives. In short, I want to convert your doubts about selling into an interest in and enthusiasm for selling. This is my goal.

My Qualifications

I expect that this book will generate the same question that my previous books [Black Folks' Guide To Making Big Money In America (1980), and Black Folks' Guide to Business Success (1986)] have generated, namely, what are my qualifications for writing a book like this. I do not have the traditional credentials that you might expect or desire. I do not have a degree in business, have never worked for a major corporation (thank goodness) and have not had a lot of experience at product sales. Yes, I have been successful at marketing my business books. But, I am not claiming that as a qualification for writing this book.

My qualifications for talking about sales to Black folks are based on over twenty years of trying *to sell Black folks on themselves.*

I have tried to say to Black America, recognize the unique gifts and talents you have to offer to the world. In the 60's and 70's these talents were most recognized in music and entertainment, sports, politics and educational achievements. In the 1980's and beyond, the unique aspects of Black-American culture must now be used to advance our efforts in business and commerce. My qualifications are grounded in my knowledge of Black-American culture. It is easy to know us as customers in the marketplace, studies are readily available. But it has not been in White America's interest to sift through the buying patterns of Blacks to find concepts which, when reversed or reinterpreted, would give clues as to how we might sell. This to me is the job of a Black writer-thinker, and I for one am going to try to carry out this responsibility.

Most Black Americans I believe, do not give enough value to their cultural distinctions, but it is very important in business. People want authenticity when they buy; they want it in the person they are buying from as well as in the product. They want French perfume, German cars, Chinese food and Black music. When something looks phony or sounds phony it just doesn't sell. We see this today in some of the "Black" commercials on television. The "Black" characters are so "White" in their expressions and mannerisms that they are not believable to the very people they are directed towards. Who buys something from someone they don't believe?

Selling success is not possible unless the salesperson has a very good understanding of who he/she is. And this is only possible if the sales person feels good about him or herself, and, radiates confidence and a sense of purpose. With all the hundreds of sales books on the market already, not one is designed to get Balck people to feel good about themselves and selling. I think I am qualified to do both. I sincerely hope this book will help you get where you want to go.

This Material - GETTING BLACK FOLKS TO SELL - can be presented in half day, full day or weekend workshops formats:

Other Business or Motivational Presentations
are Available as well

For Further Information Contact:

George Subira
Very Serious Business Enterprises
P.O. Bo 356
Newark, N.J. 07101
(609) 641-0776

An Audio Tape Cassette Program

covering the major points in *GETTING BLACK FOLKS TO SELL* will be available for purchase in the Spring of 1988. The video tape version of this material should be available in the Fall of 1988.

For further Information write to:

George Subira
Very Serious Business Enterprises
P.O. Bo 356
Newark, N.J. 07101
(609) 641-0776

ESTABLISHING THE IMPORTANCE OF SELLING SKILLS

Why is selling an extremely important skill that Black folks must learn if we are to survive and prosper in America? The first order of business of this volume is to make a strong case for the importance of selling because failing to do so would render everything else in this book virtually useless. In order to do this however, I must go over a lot of Black and American history which may at first seem completely irrelevant to selling. But if you patiently read on, the connections should clearly come together for you.

Our American Presence as Slaves and Laborers

Why are Blacks in America in the first place? Did we come to the U.S. and land on Ellis Island at the Statute of Liberty to seek religious, political or financial freedom as most other Americans did? Of course not. We came to America as part of an economic system of which a great part was slavery. So the very reason that Black people are in America has an economic foundation. From 1619 to about 1863, most Black people were forced laborers in a governmentally-approved system of slavery. After the Civil War, Black people were still viewed as laborers by both themselves and others. Farm labor, in the form of tenant farming and sharecropping, was the basic life style for the Southern-based Black community. During that time (1870's to 1920's), Black America produced many outstanding intellectuals, politicians, ministers and other professional people; yet virtually all of them were considered exceptions. The overwhelming majority of Black folks were laborers. That is how we behaved and thought as laborers.

1

When Black folk went North to Philly, New York, Baltimore, Detroit, Chicago, Boston, Cleveland, etc., we developed skills and some of us became skilled laborers. We took jobs in factories of every conceivable type and continued to work away to maintain some type of existence.

It should go without saying at this point, that Black Americans did not earn wages comparable to that of White Americans doing the same work. Sometimes we made half of what Whites did; often it was less than half.

But Black Americans survived and multiplied. During this period of time, they constantly sought ways to remedy their plight. The first strategy was to leave the overt, harsh racism of the South by moving to a northern urban area. The second major strategy was to prove our patriotism and loyalty by serving in the two World Wars. We figured America would change its views of us if we fought a common enemy side by side. So we killed and died and labored for America, but by 1950 we were still denied most of the rights that other Americans enjoyed. Meanwhile, two major organizations had formed (NAACP and The Urban League) as well as periodic mass movements (i.e., The Marcus Garvey Movement) to attack the injustices that were hurled at Black Americans. Despite much success, we were very short of our goals.

Throughout the first half of this century the essential nature of the work performed by most Black Americans could be characterized as labor. We labored in factories, in the government, in private industry and in the military. Our "educated" and "professional" ranks grew significantly during these years, but they still accounted for only a small percentage of the working masses.

The Supreme Court ruling which outlawed segregation in schools in 1954 (as well as later rulings) began to have a major impact on Black people by the 1960's. During this time the well known and successful Civil Rights Movement changed the nature of the nation and changed the way White Americans and Black Americans interacted with each other.

As opportunities began to open up, education became the final ticket out of the unskilled labor category, which up to that point had been the legacy of all of the previous generations of Black Americans.

Changes In the Nature of the American Economy

From about 1975 onward, several things started to happen that signaled a change in the economic picture in America.

Beginning with the Arab oil embargo, all oil-related products shot up in price. It was the first time that most Americans could actually see and feel how something that happened thousands of miles away, affected the way they were living at home. Inflation became a reality and people who previously had a rather casual attitude about money and the cost of goods now became very concerned with financial issues. As years went on it was obvious that oil was but one major product coming from outside the country. Japanese, Korean, and European items all found their way to the American market place and into our homes. Within 10 years, this sprinkle of foreign goods would become a flood, and whole industries would be dominated by other-than-American companies. Even worse, thousands of skilled workers and laborers alike were laid off jobs that they had thought were secure. Black workers as usual, suffered unemployment at more than twice the national rate, which had been the pattern for decades. When American companies did not go out of business for good, they often transferred the most labor intensive aspect of their operation to another country entirely where they could pay the native population much lower wages and avoid other American business expenses. Unions which used to fight for hefty raises, now just try to hold on to what they already have. Many times they agree to a pay cut to avoid losing their jobs altogether.

Great amounts of over spending and national debt by the Federal government caused a more conservative administration to sharply cut back on funding programs which they felt were ineffective or unimportant. This included many of the specially-funded government programs that had their beginning back during the more socially conscious period of the 1960's and early 1970's. Many Black folks lost their footing in the job market when these programs folded. Many had professional positions and backgrounds and had difficulty getting similar positions in the private sector.

Interest rates, or the cost of borrowing money, shot up drastically by the late seventies and thereby discouraged the housing industry (hurting those involved in the industry) and the expansion or start-up of new businesses.

The computer industry also began to flourish during that time. Because they were used as a cost saving device for both personal and business purposes, they undoubtedly had a negative impact on the lower skilled end of the general and Black labor markets.

As Black folks segregated from the main stream, we often spend so much time dealing with our frustrating personal problems and staggering community problems that we forget that there is a hell of a lot more going on in the broader world. Just because we don't keep up with these other developments doesn't mean they won't kick us in the rump a year or two down the line. On the contrary, this is exactly what has happened. Unemployment in the Black community today may be caused less by racism than by the simple fact that "the man don't need us no more".

This is not only an economic crisis for Balck America, but a *psychological crisis* as well. You see we not only have a 360 year history of earning our income from working for White folks, we also have a 360 year history of defining *who we actually are* by describing what we do for White folks. Other people in the world define who they are to the rest of the world by simply describing what they have developed in their communities or what role they play in their communities. We Black folks get our biggest charge by describing what we do for, with or in White America, "the real world". When White folks say here are your walking papers, too many of us don't just interpret that as being in need of a new source of income. Many of us interpret that as the *definition of our worthlessness*. If White folks don't need you, you feel worthless.

Worse yet, when many get kicked off the plantation that they have grown to love, they not only fail to wise up and get their own act together, but they also fall into an escapism fed by drugs and alcohol.

These then are the conditions which highlight the reasons for why Black folks need to get involved in sales.

Reasons For Blacks To Learn Selling Skills

#1. Black Labor is Becoming Obsolete

The first reason why Black people need to learn this new skill called selling is because many of their old skills are no longer useful. Black labor is quickly becoming obsolete. A 364-year tradition of *laboring* for White folks is coming to a halt not because they don't like Blacks, but because they don't need our labor. He's got machines, computers and robots to do it faster, better, cheaper and, all night long. So here we sit as Black people with a resumé listing 360 years of experience in something that is less and less needed. While this is bad enough, our children are dropping out of school at such a rate (or graduating with such poor skills) that the national employment market sees them as only qualifying for labor related positions. That means that the least desirable category of worker seems to be the very category that is expanding the fastest in our community.

How does learning to sell address these problems? Well lets look at a few things. Regardless of how many foreign goods are coming into this country, they all fit under one category; they are items which have to be sold. The more things there are to sell, the greater the need for people and companies to sell them. Secondly, selling, unlike many other professions, is much more a *response of desire* than actual skills. One could want very, very badly to be a basketball pro, a hit singer, a neuro surgeon or a governor. But, if the skills, intellect and conditions (luck) are not there, you won't make it. Virtually anyone, however, who wants to be a salesperson can become one because it is simply a matter of improving something that we all do every day. We all communicate. We all listen.

We all try to persuade. We all try to please people. Selling involves learning how to do these things better using no other tools than the ones that virtually all of us were endowed with at birth. Finally, even though the so called hard core unemployed live in the deepest parts of the ghetto, money is still there and plenty of buying is still going on. If this were not the case, people from other parts of the world wouldn't be knocking each other over in an effort to set up businesses in these so called "poor" areas.

#2. Underutilization of Black College Grads.

During my lectures around the country I ask the audiences two simple questions. First, I ask all those who know someone with a college degree who is unemployed to raise their hand. Usually, at least 25% of the group knows someone in this category. Then I ask them to raise their hands if they know a college graduate who is underemployed or working a job that doesn't require a college degree or pays less than what a college graduate would be expected to make. At least half the people in the room respond to the second question.

Often times, the audience is very surprised that so many people know underutilized Black college grads. Their surprise is based on several things. First, although a college degree is rather common these days, the percentage of American Blacks having one is still considered an achievement in most cities. To be Black, "educated", and living in an era when affirmative action hiring programs exist in thousands of companies, should virtually guarantee at least some form of employment. Well, it apparently does not. Many folks thought that the unemployed (or under employed) people that they know are *exceptions* they are either lazy, undecided or otherwise at fault for their situations. Perhaps some are. When hundreds of hands go up among audiences around the country, however, it is a clear indication that something is wrong. Or at least *it should be.*

I say should be because one would think that if a particular approach is not working, then it *should be* reexamined. For the most part, this is not happening in the Black Community. The reason for the unemployment among young, educated Blacks is always blamed on "this administration". It doesn't matter who is in office at the time, the answer is always the same.

It is my personal opinion that Black folks have a blind allegiance to the value of a college education. It is, of course, clearly understandable. A nation of Whites constantly told us how unqualified we were. Consequently, we saw college as the human mechanic shop. Whatever was wrong or unfinished with us would be fixed in college. By doing what we were told and learning what we were told for 4 years, we would reach the state of perfection called *qualified*. Of course we weren't clear as to what we would be qualified to do, but we were told over and over again to "make sure we get that piece of paper" (the degree).

But now the truth is known to almost everyone. College success is no assurance of personal or financial success. It is not even an assurance of constant employment.

Selling resolves the same dilemmas for the educated, unemployed Black American as it does for his or her less educated brothers and sisters. Just as the labor skills possessed by many unemployed laborers have become obsolete in today's economy, so too are many of the subject areas studied in college. That means non-technical, liberal arts types of studies have very little, if any, appeal to the people who do the hiring in this country. Of course, I'm sure you have probably heard a much different tune from corporate America. "We like our employees to have a broad background and understanding of the world before we train them for more specific functions within our company", they say. Sure, that reasoning applies if you are White, have a Greenwich, Connecticut address, did your undergrad work at Dartmouth and have a father with 20 years of experience in middle and/or upper management. Corporate America will assume with this background that you have had a life long indoctrination and exposure to WASP culture and values, as well as an appreciation for the intellectual process. At *that point* a corporate personnel manager may feel you are properly oriented to the corporate culture and will therefore hire you. If however, you are Black, from Harlem, and among the first generation of your family to attend college, that same personnel manager will tell *you that* you do not have the *specific skills* needed for the position. So, what they're telling you is that your A's in philosophy, sociology, English literature and the like are pointless from an employment perspective.

One of the difficulties in understanding the perspective of the Black college grad lies in not appreciating how much self-deception is part of the entire experience. When asked, "Why are you going to college", most youngsters will say "to get an education". When asked to define what education is, many are at a loss for words. When they get their "education " and then can not get hired in the real world, many become upset. When asked why they are upset they will say "because I cannot get a job". One can then remind them that they *never said* they were going to college to get a job. They said they were going "to get an education". Many young people *assumed* that a job would follow the education like night follows day. One can then remind them that they could never even define what they meant by education in the first place. It is this blind and unquestioned allegiance to the college degree and, self deception as to the purpose and usefulness of college that helps keep our graduates underutilized.

Not only do college graduates have problems finding employment, but Black professionals catch hell also. The Black professionals' problem is centered around the standardized test. To practice most professions one has to not only have the educational credentials but usually must also have a state or national license.

The situation goes something like this. When all students apply to college they usually have to submit scores from one or two national college entrance exams. Black Americans protest the use of these scores for the following reasons: First, the tests are culturally biased and are slanted to favor those who are a part of or have been exposed to WASP culture. They ignore the values and words used in minority cultures. Secondly, the tests have a poor track record in terms of predicting the future success of the minority student. Lastly, the areas covered on the exam are totally irrelevant to the students intended area of study in college. Whites eventually concede that the argument has some merit and allow Blacks with lower scores to enter school. Many of these students will graduate; some will have done very well, some will have barely gotten through, while others will have fallen completely by the wayside for any number of reasons. The same process occurs on the graduate and professional school level with similiar results.

Upon graduating from graduate or professional school are Blacks ready to practice their profession? Why yes, of course, if they can get past the old dragon they have successfully eluded so far - the standardized test.

Even though the test was required for entrance to school, the significance of the results could be de-emphasized and acceptance could still occur. But at the point of entering a profession, the situation is quite different. This next level of standard testing is to obtain a license to enter the field you were trained for during the last six to ten years of your life. This test is non-negotiable. You can no more practice law without passing the Bar exam than you can legally drive a car without a driver's license. Thus, we have lawyers who aren't "real" lawyers, doctors who can't practice medicine, accountants who aren't "certified" and a whole host of other professionals who have not yet crossed the finish line.

Even when many Black professionals do pass all of their licensing exams, they may live in cities in the nation where those types of professionals are "a dime a dozen" and may find themselves, at least temporarily, taking a position that is, in effect, *under employment*. That is, they could very well take a job that doesn't call for their skills as a lawyer, accountant or petroleum engineer. Furthermore, they may not have the salary or the prospects of a person in that profession either.

The main point here is that the under utilization of our educated folks is another reason why we need to shift our attention to the area of sales. The pursuit of college degrees does not ensure that we will be able to make a decent living even when we jump over all the hurdles that are placed in our path. The mood, the bank accounts and the general predicament of too many of our educated folks is a mirror image of our uneducated ones. Selling, on the other hand, is a profession that is so universally intertwined with the total nature of how the nation operates, it would be impossible for any one agency, institution or regulatory body to prevent us from using those basic skills in one field or another. Highly educated folks may have looked down their noses at salespeople in the past but today they had better realize that many people in sales have more freedom, income and status than those in more traditional professions.

#3 *To Bring More Income into the Black Community*

The Black community boasts an economy in 1987 of over two hundred billion dollars and predictions abound as to how much income this community will have by the year 2000 (some predict as much as 800 billion dollars). Though these figures are impressive, we need to look at the details behind the figures.

For about as long as the census bureau has kept records, the average Black worker has been paid from between 55 to 61 cents for every dollar paid to the average White worker. In this era of two hundred billion dollar incomes, we *still* make less than two-thirds of the income of the average White worker. The two hundred billion dollars often referred to is only about 7.6 percent of the nation's total income and Black Americans comprise at least 11.5 percent of the nation's population. In other words, the Black community needs at least 50 percent more income than it is currently receiving (that comes to over *100 billion dollars*) before we can start to feel that there is economic parity in this country.

The methods of generating Black income have been referred to previously and include labor, civil service, and corporate positions, skilled trades and the professions. Hundreds of thousands of people have had fruitful lives utilizing these strategies to secure income. But virtually ignored in the overall favorable strategy of income improvement has been the area of sales. The instances of local community groups, churches or traditional civil rights organizations training Black youngsters and/or adults in sales is almost non-existent. Thus, we have never been able to develop a tradition in selling and this has hurt us.

Today, the corporate giants that were once relied upon to hire people are themselves shrinking. The number of people hired now is significantly less than a decade ago. The average citizen views economic growth today in terms of the opening of malls, franchise businesses and small, private concerns.

But if you look at the nature of the work force of many of these newly established small businesses, you will see a pattern. They are principally minimum wage workers supervised by a low-salaried manager in an environment that calls for the workers to do the same simple functions over and over again. The questions the Black community has to ask itself are: Is this type of economic growth going to help us catch up in the struggle for economic equality? Can we catch up if we are paid the lowest wages allowable by law? Is this simply a guarantee that Black folks will always be at the bottom of the economic ladder? The other question one has to ask is how often does the minimum wage increase? As I write this in 1987 I can tell you it has been *years* since the minimum wage has budged and I have heard more discussion about lowering the minimum wage than I have heard about raising it.

The only way Black America can increase it's money supply to eventually make it possible to get 100 percent of its fair share is to: A) enter an income situation where there is no automatic limit or ceiling on the allowable income, and B) get more money that is now in the possession of the White community into our community.

The field of selling addresses both needs. First in the case of income, if you are paid by commission (that is you earn a percentage of all that you sell) and if there are no limits placed on how much you can sell, then there would be no limits on what your commission income could be. Example: if you sell real estate and you sell a house every other day (if you could do it) then you could get a very healthy pay check every other day as well. This is also called performance based income. The better you perform, the better the pay. This is not the case in most jobs that most people work, Black or White.

Secondly, selling allows Black salespeople to sell to the White community (or any community for that matter). If we get involved in selling to corporate America its computer systems, phone systems, copy machines, employee benefit packages etc. we become vehicles through which money is passed between the two communities. Since Black America cannot print its own money, the only viable way we can increase the money in our community is to bring it in from an outside community. This should sound so basic and common as to be almost ridiculous. But do you realize that the overwhelming majority of the Black community either does not realize it or is not acting on what they know to be true. In my mind one situation is as bad as the other.

#4 Better Opportunities To Get Past the Screening Process.

To be denied a job that one feels perfectly qualified and prepared to perform in one of the most frustrating experiences encountered in job hunting. This situation happens to everyone, but due to racism in this country it occurs more often to Black Americans than to the majority population. While it is easy to legitimately cry *racism* in these situations, it is also constructive to occasionally look over the fence at the other guys point of view for a more balanced perspective.

In the first place, an individual should know that no one person controls the number of jobs allowed in a particular company as much as general and specific *economic conditions* dictate the growth rate of jobs. When times are good, jobs are plentiful and when conditions turn sour, employment may not only cease but layoffs may occur. Often times, Black folks, (generally feeling a sense of powerlessness anyway), assume that no matter what the circumtances, White folks are always in control. It is important to understand that they too are often the victims of surprises, plots and plans. But it makes our job as angry Blacks so much easier to point to one person or group of persons and say "you guys are responsible for two million employable Black folks being out of work." But that is not possible because nobody has that much power over the entire commercial market of the nation. This is especially true today since the Japanese, Koreans, Tiwanese, West Germans and English have more to say about some American industries than Americans themselves.

So the first point I want to make clear is that if you are having difficulty landing a job, there is little likelihood that a bad man boogie man is hiding somewhere waiting "to get you" and your people or keep you from working. Powerful men and women in certain companies in certain, small communities may seem to be in such a position. But generally speaking, job growth responds to worldwide, national, regional and local conditions, not specific people.

In those instances where there *are* job openings, a company's personnal department almost always has a screening process of some kind. The screening process is designed to help a company make the best hiring decision (from their point of view, not yours). It is during the screening process that Black folks get taken off the track and are therefore stopped in *their* tracks from getting the position they seek.

The screening process is not only an analysis of a person's educational and experiential background, but an investigation into one's life style, habits, and values as well. When a company hires someone, more than just a skilled employee comes to work. A whole person with a range of beliefs, viewpoints and behavior patterns enters the work place every day and impacts the effectiveness of other workers. So it is both valuable and practical for a company to look very closely at prospective employees because a partnership of sorts (some even say a marriage) begins when a person is hired. If this is not clear to you right now, it will become very, very clear when you have your own company and begin to look to hire your own employees/ partners.

Because racism is present in all aspects of American life (not just the work place) many Black people, at one time or another in their lives, have responded strongly or made statements against it. Consequently, they may have blemished their backgrounds and their work records. Some workers may have unexpectedly quit a job, cursed out or struck a worker or supervisor who made a racist remark, or have been involved in some other such incident.

Since there is also a strong relationship between racism, poverty and crime, many Black workers have other "blemishes" in their backgrounds. They may surface in military, police, medical or educational records. America requires Black folks not only to endure racism, but also to do so peaceably. When they show resistance to or attack the many manifestations of rascism, Balck folks are either labelled "agitators" or they develop a reputation for "breaking the peace".

The personnel director at most companies is usually not Black. They should not be expected to have a completely sympathetic and accurate understanding of the history of racism in America. They are only employees themselves doing what they are being told, in an effort to earn promotions and raises. The better they screen out undersirables and hire "good people" the more brownie points they earn. It's nothing personal.

The bottom line result of all this is that Black folks, who are otherwise qualified to do a job, get screened out of the selection process because of the kinds of blemishes already mentioned. Additionally, they may be eliminated for the following reasons: a poor credit report, frequent relocations, (supposedly a sign of instability), the absence of letters of recommendation or referral, a poor score on the screening exam, and dress and grooming habits. When there are at least four times as many people applying for a position as there are openings, it takes very little for an interviewer to screen out an individual. This has been our legacy in the job world.

Now, how does the world of sales differ from all that has been mentioned above? Well, realistically speaking there are many, many different types of sales positions. In the corporate environment, sales companies are every bit as strict in the screening process as other companies, in some cases, even more so.

Since however, every single thing is for sale in this country, there are plenty of situations where one will not be screened out.

In direct sales companies (also known as door-to-door sales, multi-level sales, home party plan sales, etc.), there is very little concern about one's previous history. Information concerning criminal records, school grades, test scores, drug usage or credit history is rarely, if ever, requested. These companies are mainly concerned with how well you perform in your relationship with them. If you pay for your products up front and operate, not in their facilities, but in the same environment in which you live, there is less concern about your history because you pose very little threat to the company. This isn't to say that sales companies take no precautions as to how they are represented to the public. Every organization has a set of rules and regulations which when broken or ignored, may be grounds for dismissal. In a way, this is *true* justice. Rather than being labeled guilty because of past transgressions, you are considered innocent, in some sales organizations you until you prove otherwise.

Many of these same principles would also apply if you started your own company. When dealing with suppliers and wholesalers, they could care less if you smoked pot, had half a dozen children out of wedlock or failed to make it through high school. As long as you treated them "fair and square", your personal background wouldn't matter.

To review what has been presented here, I'd like to repeat the following points. Selling is an important skill for the Black community to learn because it allows us to respond to being screened out of the traditional means of making an income-the job. Personnel interviewers have a responsibility to their companies to hire the best people; they can afford to be choosy because there usually are at least three or more times the number of applicants than actual openings. Due to Black America's exposure to poverty, racism and crime, as well as assumptions about values and life styles uncommon to the White majority, we are often screened out of many available jobs, even when we are "qualified" for the positions. Many companies, however, do not use screening tests and applications, but instead give all individuals an even start. As long as one follows the guidelines and adequately performs in the selling of products, he/she is allowed to make an income regardless of past mistakes. 'Nuff said on this point.

#5 Less Discrimination In Income Through Sales

It was previously stated that the typical Black worker makes 58 to 61 percent of the salary of the typical White worker. There are two reasons why this difference in income develops. First, White Americans are given the better paying jobs within a given company. When one realizes that companies are often owned by the very people who make the higher salaries, one would have to conclude that even without racism, a certain amount of salary differential is unavoidable. Secondly, White people are paid a higher salary for the same job performed by Black workers of equal status and ability. This is more clearly discrimination based on race (or racism). Selling can serve as an income equalizer. If wholesale and retail prices are equal for both races then profit margins will also be equal.

In other words, if people of different races work for the same company and sell cars, airplane tickets, computers, pianos, stereo systems, etc., for the same retail price, then there is a much greater chance that each person, regardless of race, will make the same margin of profit. Thus, salespeople have a better opportunity to make more equal incomes than those working in salaried positions. Of course, actual, final incomes will vary based on how much each person sells. The point to be made is that when the commission percentage are clear and above board, the opportunity for equal pay is much more likely.

#6 Keeping The Dollar In the Black Community

In the era of the '80's, it has been quite popular to talk about the economic development of the Black community. One of the most common rallying cries is that Black folks should spend their money in their own community. Currently, only about 6 percent of Black income is spent with Black businesses which means that 94 percent is spent in the general market. The basic motivation behind this drive is a good one and I have no doubt that all the proponents of this idea are well intentioned. The one basic flaw in this thinking, however, is that there is the assumption that Black folks are *selling* the things we need and this is not true. If you were to look through the "Black Pages" (a listing of local Black businesses) of even some major cities (over 250,000 Blacks in the Metro area), you will find that the range of businesses (salespeople) you could patronize in those areas are very limited. Most types of balck business in the 1980's are the same as those that existed in the 1960's, namely, beauty and barber shops, small construction componies, liquior stores and bars, security companies, grocery stores and restaurants, janitorial, secretarial services, etc. Of course one or two car dealerships, and franchises of various kinds exist in large cities. But you would be surprised at what doesn't exist. In my travels, for instance, I have never encountered a Black-owned stereo store with top of the line stereo equipment, including the various Japanese imports. What is more basic to the average Black household than a stereo system, or for that matter, a stove, refrigerator, washer and dryer, furniture and other high ticket items. The point I am making is that Black people must get involved in *selling* if the idea of holding the dollar in the Black community is ever going to have any meaning. You can't buy from somebody if they aren't selling what you need. So we must at least begin to sell if people are to have the opportunity to buy from us.

An issue that comes up every so often concerns Black salespeople in White stores. Well of course we need to support Black salespeople in White stores because usually this is where they begin to sharpen their skills. Only after they develop a solid list of customers, gain knowledge of their respective industries, and establish credibility with suppliers can Black salespeople justify to themselves the risk of opening up their own establishments. As much as everyone would like to see new Black businesses pop up like dandelions, if the potential owners do not have excellent selling, promotional and marketing skills, they will, in all likelihood, be quickly out of business.

#7 *Broader Opportunities For Income and Self-Realization*

Thirty years ago, the social levels in the Black community, were very narrowly defined. You were either a professional (i.e., doctor, lawyer, dentist, minister, funeral parlor director, or teacher), or you worked in a farming, civil service or labor position. The overwhelming majority of our people fit into one of these categories, however, there were numerous exceptions.

In the '80's Black folks are doing or are on the verge of doing everything. Blacks have become astronauts, Miss America, big city mayors, top models, and TV stars. The opportunities for them to participate in the broader scope of American life has multiplied in recent years. But one thing that has multiplied faster than anything else in this country is the number of products people can buy. It is more important that we have more people to *sell* these products than simply adding to the numbers of actors, models, astronauts, etc. It is absolutely incredible what companies, both foreign and domestic, have developed to make people spend (waste) their money. Not only have the *number* of products increased but the variety of products including styles and brands, has also drastically risen. When I was very young, I, and many other young boys could name most automobiles on sight. Not today. There are more varieties of cars and price ranges than the average person could ever hope to see. When I get my baggage from an airline terminal, seldom, even among hundreds of bags, will I see two that are exactly alike. All of these things have one thing in common, they have to be sold. They are not given away. Since White America has seen, and in large part, accepted our expanded participation in society (e.g., mayors, network news anchors, ambassadors, etc.) they will accept us as salespersons, especially if we are good.

What does this mean to the average Black person? It means many things or at least it should. It means that you can be somebody, and live a good life from a good income.

#8 Your First Chance or Your Last Chance To Be a Professional

Words have importance; and powerful words mean a great deal. (If you don't believe it, call your mother or father a string of four-letter words and see how they respond to you). One of the realities for Black Americans has been, over several decades, the struggle for *acceptance.*; not only by White folks but also by each other. In the Black community one sure way of gaining *status* and *acceptance* was to become a *professional*. We can debate the merits of whether it is in the best interest of the Black community to cater to their professionals at the expense of their non-professionals, but for right now it really doesn't matter. This is the way it is. The situation today was set in motion many years ago and if it does change it will take many years of gradual reappraisal.

For people who are *taught not* to feel good about themselves, especially the way they look, talk, and think, there is a need to find a means of acceptance. They need to learn to accept themselves, and feel accepted by their own community and society at large. A key to that process is the development within each individual a sense of pride, status and professionalism. The sales field offers the person who will not become a doctor, lawyer, dentist, or whatever, a chance to become a professional in something. For many Black folks it may be their first chance. For other Black folks who want to leave teaching, the ministry or social work, it may provide the opportunity for them to continue to be identified with the "class" of persons called professionals. And for the college drop out, ex criminal offender, reformed alcoholic or junkie, the sales field can be their last chance in life to enter that group they call the "professionals".

The fact that most people in the Black community don't` recognize salespeople as professionals is mostly a signal of our lack of exposure to the business world. It is also a situation that I think is changing as we get more involved in the area of business.

The fundamental point to be understood here is that we as a people have a knee jerk response of *no* when asked if the opportunities for

Blacks are improving in America. The truth is that as long as we ignore one of the greatest areas of opportunities-sales-we will never really recognize opportunity, much less take advantage of it.

#9 Constant Employment and Mobility

I have said on many occasions that I know of two kinds of people. The first kind complains about the fact that they don't have a jobs. The second group complains about the jobs that they do have. Both situations are quite understandable. The difficulty of Black Americans getting hired is well known. Thus, it is easy to see why many accept what ever opportunity comes their way. On the other hand because Blacks and other minorities are often forced to take the lowest paying, and most boring and dangerous jobs that exist, it is also easy to see why they complain about such positions. If both situations are so easily understandable it seems as if many Black folks are doomed to live a life they hate because of the sheer struggle of it all. If you ask around that is exactly what tens of thousands of people are doing. They know they need a source of income but they hate the one that they have. They don't feel as if they can move on to a better position because the skills they have acquired on the present job relate mostly to the performance of that job. It's called a deadend situation, and many people know exactly what it is because they are in it and have been for years.

Developing skills in the area of sales is a way out of a dead-end situation for several reasons. First of all, the skills learned and the processes involved in selling are fairly standard, no matter what is being sold. Therefore once a person has learned the sales process, cold, they are more than likely in a position to sell just about anything. The skills applied in selling cars can be transfered to selling houses, or appliances or furniture. Does that mean that a good salesperson can sell anything as has been often stated. Probably not, since a key to selling is the degree of faith or love a salesperson has for their product and one cannot love all things equally. But the fact is, unlike many training programs which are good for just one or two things, selling success means mobility, options and constant employment. The day you open a newspaper in any town in America and not see ads for salespeople is the day the earth will come to an end. It will never happen in our lifetime. The demand for good salespeople is constant and great. Many of the positions request experience in selling a particular item; but, a good salesperson can overcome that requirement by "selling" the new employer on the wealth of experience he/she will bring to the new job, and the reasons for wanting the opportunity to sell the new employer's product. Black America particularly needs to put itself in a position of having access to constant employment. So many of our families, communities and neighborhoods have been broken apart because of poor finances, it would be a refreshing change to have consistent employment and the option of using our skills wherever we desired without feeling trapped by or tied to a company, town or state. This is part of what I call freedom.

#10 Transferable Skills

The skills learned in product sales are not only transferable within the field itself but are also of great benefit outside that arena. Why is this so? Because everyone has to sell themselves everyday to the people with whom they meet and work. When you open your mouth, you are asking people to be persuaded by your ideas, thoughts and feelings on a subject. There are some occupations that call for selling skills more than others. The politician, for example, has to be persuasive, and articulate to win the confidence of the public at large. They have to get you to listen to their eloquent persentations and to act (vote). Furthermore a politician has to respond to people who disagree with their point of view (handle objections). Sales skills are also very important when seeking financing from a bank. You have to sell a bank on your product, your market, your projections, your collateral and yourself. Failure to sell the banker will often keep you from getting the opportunity to sell the public. Selling skills even help you in your personal life in terms of negotiating with your spouse, children or other relatives. Meeting new people is usually easier for a salesperson than a nonsales type. Generally speaking, being a successful salesperson helps you to "get your way" and wouldn't most of us like ot have our own way whenever we could get it.

#11 The Best Pool For Future Business Leaders

Several articles in the last few years have made it a point to say that the values of college students in the 80's is much different than those of college students in the 60's. Students of the 80's want money, status, security and plenty of adult toys. It should be no surprise that this interest in money coincides with a great upsurge in the number of Black and White students majoring in business. Many White students have the advantage of early exposure to and understanding of business. When they hear pure theory in the classroom, many can recognize it from the reality of the business world. Black students on the other hand, take business courses without clarity of purpose and can't always make distinctions between theory and reality. Because colleges have as its basic objective the preparation of workers (or at least people who think like workers) and because Black folks are overwhelming workers as a group, the Black business student will, for all intents and purposes, wind up as a worker in a formal (maybe corporate) business environment. What this means is that there is very little relationship between Black students who are "educated" in business and the number of these students who actually do start or plan their own businesses. This is a very crucial reason why the Black community needs tens of thousands of people actively involved in sales. *Salespeople, not college people, form the best pool of candidates for future business owners.* Salespeople do what business owners do, they sell the product.

As was stated earlier, Blacks usually start out selling for White companies often with no preplanned notion of starting a business. If they become good at selling, develop a liking for it, and see the money that they are earning for their employers, it usually doesn't take long for them picture themselves in their own enterprises.

WHY BLACK AMERICANS HAVE NEGLECTED THE SALES FIELD

In the previous chapter, I presented some concrete reasons why the Black American community should now turn its efforts towards the sales field. I hope that regardless of your background, educational level or political ideology, you see a great deal of merit in those reasons. If you have been convinced of the importance of selling, several questions may be forming in your mind right now. For example, if selling is so basic to the development of our community and its people, how come we as a people are not doing it? How come our various leaders are not discussing the benefits of sales and the development of selling skills? Why do Black folks shy away from selling?

These and similar questions will be addressed in this chapter. Understand, however, that other references will be made throughout the book as to why there has been a reluctance on the part of Black folks to become involved in sales.

Reason #1 - The Historical Momentum of Our Labor History.

One cannot deny the incredible impact that 300 years of slavery has had on the development of the thinking, the culture, and the outlook of today's Black American community. There is a law of physics that says that an object in motion tends to stay in motion unless acted upon by an outside force. The Black community, which historically worked in labor-related jobs has a natural tendency to continue in that direction unless specifically acted upon by an outside force.

Although the Civil War and the Northern migrations from the South definitely changed our lifestyles and work patterns, it is only recently, as the need for labor lessens, that the issue of changing our work habits can be seen as one of clear-cut survival.

Reason #2 - Lack of Proper Role Models.

In the Black Community, we do not have very many successful salespeople as positive role models. Many times when we see people selling, we give them negative labels, such as hustler, beggar, huckster and the like. Role models are important because you can't expect people to aspire to that which they cannot see or conceive. Thus, teachers, parents, friends, and neighbors of young people rarely encourage them to enter the sales field because they are themselves unaware of very many success stories.

One reason for the lack of development of positive role models in sales is the position of the media. The media in this country, in both the Black and White communities, consistently focuses on the giants of the entertainment industry or the sensation of crime and other such things. In the Black media, for example, there is a tremendous amount of attention given to the lifestyles of entertainers, sports figures and politicians. If, however, the Black community attempted to find an article on successful salespeople, they would probably have a hard time finding such an article. Therefore, even when successful role models do exist in the business world, the fact that they are not covered by the media makes them virtually unknown to the people who need to know about them.

The situation is practically the same when it comes to White news publications, newspapers and magazines. Here, the emphasis is very often on the criminal acts committed by the Black community.

Reason #3 - Uncreative Approaches by Black Leadership

It is important to understand that in the beginning stages of the recognition of Black leaders in this country, they were never called leaders, originally, but spokespeople. And what a spokesperson basically did was articulate the will of the masses that he/she represented. Thus, if the masses had, as their goal, the increase of jobs, then that is what, in fact the spokesperson would say to the White powers that be; the masses have an interest in the development of more jobs.

As times and circumstances changed, however, and leaders became more sophisticated, it was up to them to express not just the will of the masses, but to come up with creative solutions to problems that hopefully, they were better able to analyze than the the masses. If this had been done, I think we would have seen an earlier emphasis on the development of businesses and the selling skills necessary to make those businesses successful. This should have been on the agendas of newly emerging leaders, at least in the second part of the 20th century. Unfortunately, many leaders stuck to the notion of simply articulating the will of the people, thereby putting very little emphasis on the development of businesses and selling skills.

I consider this to be a lack of insight, creativity or analytical thinking on the part of Black leadership. If, in fact, Black leaders merely articulate the will of the masses that they are purporting to lead, then their thinking is no further along than the masses. If this is true, then in fact leaders are not leading; they are not really providing a new direction to a people who are in need of one.

Reason #4 - Myths, Assumptions and Half-truths About the Sales Field.

I think it is important to understand that because there were so few role models in the Black community in sales their image of the salesperson came from the White community. But, I think it is also very important to understand that the image that we obtained from the White community about what constituted a salesperson was based on how they sold to Black people, and not how they necessarily sold to their own people. Thus, over the years, alot of unfavorable myths about sales and images of salespeople have developed. They include the following:

a. *The Con Artist* - a person who has a faulty or overpriced product, but who feels so confident in his/her ability to persuade and make false promises of a particular product, that he/she can get the money out of an unsuspecting customer.

b. *The Born Salesman* - there are alot of people who feel that the ability to sell, like height, weight and eye color, is inborn. It is a natural gift and those who are not blessed with such a gift could never be a successful salesperson. This myth contributes to the lack of Blacks investigating the field of sales as a potential career option.

c. *The Need for Start-up Money* - the need for start-up money is not required to learn sales. I think it is clear that if you begin as an employee, you can learn selling skills and work on the basis of commission or a salary.

d. *White People Will Not Support Your Business*- there is a belief on the part of the Black community, that if you as a Black person, develop selling skills and have a product to sell at a reasonable price, that the White community will not support you.

I think, historically speaking, this is a very valid assumption. But, I do think that in the 1980's (and certainly beyond) the situation is different. We have to understand that the image of the Black salesperson is intertwined with the image of Black people overall. Today, White America sees Black men and women as highly-elected and appointed public officials, college presidents, newscasters and corporate managers. I think we have to appreciate that this has an impact on their perception of Black professionals generally including the Black salesperson.

I think that today, more so than in past times, the ability to sell to the White community has alot to do with making them feel comfortable in doing business with us, which has a lot to do with the amount of expertise we've gained as salespeople. This does not mean that there aren't plenty of racists still in America who would not want to do business with us on any condition. Nor does it change the fact that, if given the opportunity to buy a product from a group of people they are more familiar with than Blacks, they would more be inclined to chose the former.

e. *The Black Community Will Not Support You* - many people are reluctant to get involved in sales, not because they have any intent of ever pursuing the dollar in the White community, but because of their concern that they would get little, if any support from the Black community. This is an uncomfortable topic to talk about, but it is one that must be confronted.

The fact of the matter is that, as Black Americans, we have been taught the superiority of anything White and the inferiority of anything Black. Therefore, it is true that in many instances the Black community has not supported its own salespeople. However, I think this is the case sometimes because Black salespeople do not put as much effort into their presentations because they automatically expect a sale, in many instances, *simply because* the client they are talking to is Black.

No customer likes to be taken for granted. No customer likes to feel that they owe a particular business or person any type of special treatment. This is a problem in the Black community that has to be overcome, and it is exactly why I feel the entire spectrum of selling has to be examined.

Reason #5 - Very Poor Attitudes About Selling

As a result of poor role models and a belief in the myths about sales, we developed a bad attitude about selling as an occupation. I have always stressed the importance of the right attitude in our quest for business success but it was never made more plain to me than in 1983 while listening to a young lady give a seminar on selling.

She asked the audience two questions. They were two very simple questions, but the results were dramatic. The first question she asked was, "What are the characteristics of successful people?" The following responses came from the audience:

They are organized	They are self-reliant
They have positive attitudes	They are hard working
They are professional	They are what they do
They have a good appearance	They are goal oriented
They are good communicators	They show enthusiasm
They are independent thinkers	They have confidence
They are persistent	They are consistent

After writing the responses on the blackboard, the salestrainer asked the audience to categorize their responses. She told the group to go down the list with her and indicate which characteristics were attitudes and which were skills. Well, down the list they went and when they were finished only 3 of the 14 attributes had "SK" next to it for skill. They were: being organized, being professional in your efforts and being a good communicator.

The other 11 attributes were all considered attitudes rather than skills. The final conclusion was that for most things in life, it is not the education and training which lead to skills that are most important but the *attitude* you bring with the skills you've acquired. This is especially true in selling.

I would like to refer to page 56 of my book <u>Black Folks Guide To Business Success.</u> On this page I compare the typical attitudes of Whites successfully involved in sales with the typical negative attitudes that many, if not most, Black folks have regarding sales. Seven contrasting attitudes are listed below.

page 56 - <u>Black Folks Guide To Business Success</u>

White Attitude Toward Sales	Black Attitude Toward Sales
Selling is a great source of income; money is *everywhere*.	You go broke selling; *nobody* has any money
I don't want any *limit* put on how much money I can make.	I *need* a set salary so I can see where I'm going
I'm going to *learn* all I can about this product and the market and make a mint.	I don't have the *gift of gab* to make it in sales.
The reason I like this field is because *I in* really *independent*. I make most of the decisions as long as I bring in the bottom line.	I can be a good worker, just *tell me what to do* and I'll do it.
You know once you learn how to sell it's almost *impossible to be unemployed*; there are always openings in sales.	The people I know is sales *can't be doing that great*; every time you look up, they're selling something different
This field is great; I deal with people from *all over the world*-the Middle East, Africa, India, especially Japan and South Korea.	Hey, you know you can't make any money dealing with White Folks; they *only spend it among themselves*.
I started with that *desk full of applications* and thirty-five dollars in my pocket. Now I guess you can say I'm rich.	Well you know what *they always say*, it takes money to make money.

Obviously, it would be grossly unfair for me to lead anyone to believe that all Whites fit into their side of the column and all Blacks into theirs. There are, in fact, hundreds of thousands, probably millions, of Whites who think exactly like Blacks on the issue of sales. And there are probably a few thousand Blacks who view the opportunities in sales much like the rest of the business community. But the point is true, I think, that Black America does suffer from a strong anti-sales bias Unfortunately, this bias has blinded us to the means by which people, who did not have money, got into a position of having alot of money.

Reason #6 - A Blind Belief in College Education

This problem was discussed rather thoroughly in the previous chapter. However, it is important to understand that sales, like any other profession and any other field, grows and responds to talented people. If in fact, talented people are shuttled away from sales, it stands to reason that the development of role models is much more difficult. Consequently, it leaves the field open to representation by Con artist personalities.

Reason #7 - Lack of Proper Training

There are many people who do not take seriously the idea that selling is a profession. They developed this idea because there doesn't appear to be much in the way of educational qualifications to enter the sales field, nor are they aware of the kind of extensive training people get once they become salespeople. Most people who enter the field will tell you that selling is, in fact, a profession that requires specific techniques and practice in those techniques; failure to do so will lead to financial ruin.

Unfortunately, Black folks have not gotten much in the way of sales training. For those who did, they were not always able to make it more valid or understandable to the Black community. Obviously, without good training one will probably fail in sales, and when one fails in sales, he/she often abandons the field altogether.

Thus, many Black people view selling as a high-risk venture. The sad fact is that the people who do fail, in many instances, never get the proper training to be successful in the first place.

Reason #8 - Lack of Belief in the Product Being Sold

Closely associated with the lack of training and sales failure is a lack of belief in the product being sold. Many people get involved in sales positions out of a sense of desperation or naivete. They look for a particular job, but the job is not available. Along comes a sales recruiter with a new product promising them a lot of money. They take the position convinced that they are on their way to riches. The sales recruiter may tell them that the product is in high demand or that it will be in high demand, and that they stand to make a lot of money with this "ground floor opportunity."

In many cases, however, the salesperson has never personally used the product; is not that familiar with its features; and perhaps, is not quite comfortable with the price of the product. He/she may feel the product is overpriced, especially if it is not well made. Yet, this person enters the marketplace and tries to sell the product. It is no wonder why these kinds of people often find failure in sales.

Selling is a field that involves the conveyance of feelings and beliefs. If a person does not feel and believe that his/her product is necessary, is fairly priced, or is within the potential customers budget, then it will be very difficult to make many sales. Yet, this is the position in which many people have found themselves in past sales experiences.

Today when you ask a former salesperson about selling, he/she immediately remembers the negative situations without fully understanding the reason for them.

Reason #9 - A Fluctuating Income

Many people do not want to enter the sales field because it is notoriously a feast or famine situation. Those people who work a nine-to-five have a steady salary they can depend on to pay their bills and to buy other necessities. They are very reluctant to enter a field, regardless of the purported opportunities, that is characterized by periods of high, low, or no income. This fear, I believe, is based not only on people's genuine concern about the seasonal aspects of sales, but also on an individual's insecurity about setting up a budget, and living on that budget. They don't believe they can save money during the good times in order to have money available when times are lean.

Clearly, if a person is absolutely convinced that he/she will never have that much financial self-control, then perhaps *he/she should not enter the sales field*. However, there are many people who say that there are no real reasons for having very low periods if you are, in fact, a true and professional salesperson.

Reason #10 - Lack of Self-Confidence

The most fundamental aspect of racism that Black Americans experience is the fact that they are held out to be different and inferior to the rest of the people we refer to as Americans. In spite of the fact that a number of positive steps have been made in this country to kill the threat of racism, deeply imbedded within the consciousness of millions of Blacks, is still a feeling of inferiorty. Black people have a distinct feeling that the way they look, the way they dress, the way they talk, etc., is not widely accepted by the majority population in thus country.

For this reason, it should not be at all surprising that there is a lack of confidence on the part of Black Americans to present themselves to the rest of America. It is very much like any immigrant group that, does not speak English. They feel much more comfortable in a community where they can rely on the use of their own language to be understood and to communicate.

To a degree, a similar feeling permeates the Black community and prevents them from really feeling comfortable about making a sales presentation to the majority population. I think I am on fair ground by saying that this is particularly true of Black men. The media does such a good job at reporting crime that a Black man is perceived by both the Black community and other communities as someone you should fear and distrust. So, it is not at all uncommon for Black men to respond negatively to the idea of selling.

When a person enters the sales profession, he/she already has a track record, and a history of interaction and communication. Clearly, a person's background will dictate the degree of his/her self-confidence. Early successes in school, church, clubs, the neighborhood and socializing will help shape a person's self-image. That self-image will help influence that person to enter the sales field or not. The message that needs to be gotten out to the Black community, loud and clear, is that confidence is something that can be built up and/or restored for those who lack it or have lost it.

The interesting thing about the sales field is that, while it requires self-confidence to be successful, it is also a tool that can be used to build self-confidence. Selling develops the person who is doing the selling.

These, then, are some of the reasons why the Black community has been reluctant to investigate sales. I think it is important for you, the reader, to review these reasons to see what, if any, clues can be gained as to your own reluctance to enter the field. It is certainly not an exhaustive list of reasons why Black Americans shy away from sales, but it is a beginning.

Most of the people who need this book will not go to the Bookstore and Buy it
But They Will Buy It From You

Order at least ten copies of our materials and offer them to your circle of friends and contacts

See Page 211 For Further Directions

UNDERSTANDING THE FEAR
OF FAILURE AND OF SUCCESS

The previous section briefly outlined some specific reasons why many Black Americans may be avoiding the challenge of a sales career. In all likelihood, most individuals can identify with not just one, but several of the reasons listed. If this is true, then it should be easy to understand that the resistance to selling in the Black community is strong because there are so many factors acting in unison to prevent them from doing it.

Underlying the specific road blocks previously stated are the fears common to all classes and races of people, the fear of failure and of success. I would like to develop these two concepts not because they are so universal, but because I think they have an even greater impact on the Black community than on the general population. I also think that Black folks can reframe or reshape their views about their fears if they want to overcome them.

The Fear of Failure

The fear of failure usually has its beginning during the childhood of the person experiencing the fear. According to psychologists, the nurturing and raising of children in the U.S. is dominated by parents who put restrictions on them. Children are constantly told what they cannot do, where they cannot go and what they cannot see or ask. The threats and/or punishment for breaking the rules leads to a form of mental conditioning called negative reinforcement. It is said that one of the most common words a child fears while growing up is *the word no*. But negative reinforcement is much more than hearing the word no.

In most households when the rules are broken the *punishment* is either physical or emotional. But when a child does the *right* thing, there is very often no *reward*. This means that most children *learn to fear failing* (failing in their behavior, failing in school, failing to do household duties, etc.) because of the punishment that is almost always immediately associated with it. The greater the punishment or trauma for failure, the greater the fear for the thing leading to the punishment. For example, let's say a child is punished because of poor grades and poor grades are caused by poor test results. Perhaps a fear of tests is developed because they are the link between the child's educational efforts and his/her punishment. The final result could very well be that the fear of tests causes poor performance on tests. If the child continues to be punished for poor grades resulting from poor tests he/she will probably rebel in some way (such as quitting school) and will more than likely hate and fear tests for the rest of his/her life. This is the essence of negative reinforcement and it is standard procedure in millions of families all over the nation. The other side of this situation is when a child does well on his/her tests, and is *not* rewarded. If there is no reward for not failing (being a success), then a child doesn't learn to respond to the positive because there is no positive reinforcement. There is only the negative to respond to (via fear) because that is all that is ever presented. In this set of circumstances a child is actually *learning to be a loser* because he/she is not being given any incentive to win (no reward for success). The punishment for failing (losing) causes fear, which helps in many instances, to ensure continued poor performance. A situation like this can just as easily be played out for adults in the work place as for the child in the home. Whereas these situations and conditions cross all racial, class and religious lines, I think it is important to see how the fear of failure operates in the Black community and how it specifically shapes our attitude towards selling.

The concept of negative reinforcement is firm in the Black community and I think it's fair to say that most Black children have grown up under this type of conditioning. I believe this is so not because Black parents are harsher in their punishment than White parents, but because of the general absence of rewards for doing well. In schools in the Black community, the star athlete, the fancy dresser or dancer and the attractive person gets stroked and respected. Conversely, the good student may not get stroked. Furthermore, they may be ridiculed for being egg heads, punks or the like. Intellectual boys are particularly viewed as less masculine or effeminate, while both boys and girls are accused of "acting white" when they achieve in the classroom. Also, there is often an absence of reward from the broader community as well. In a White suburban school, the highest-ranking students often receive scholarships to the top colleges even if their parents could easily afford to pay for their education. In a "Black school" in the ghetto, the top students may be denied not only a scholarship to the top colleges, but also admission by those colleges and universities because of low standard test scores and the general reputation of inner city public schools. So what incentive is there for a young person to strive for academic excellence? In the ghetto, if a child is known to have an income from a job of some kind, it is quite possible that they may be fearful of having that money taken from them by bullies and gangs. What's even worse is that these bullies often threaten more physical harm if they are reported to any type of authority figure. Where is the incentive to continue working?

The positive reinforcement concept has taken a long vacation from the Black community in recent years. Today's problem is *more* than just negative reinforcement. Today, there has been a *reinterpretation of success* and status so that the bad guys are the good guys and the nice guys finish last. In today's ghetto environment, members of gangs have instilled fear not only in their peers but also in their teachers as well. The hoodlums drive the cars, dress in fine clothes and get the ladies because of income derived from dope sales, burglarizing of homes and businesses and stealing old ladies' pocketbooks. In the classroom, the student who cannot read and has lost interest in learning is "successfully" promoted to the next grade just as those who wrestle with homework every night. Where is the justice in all of this? In today's environment, young ladies are pressured for sex way before they can handle it, or they risk being considered a non-person or an untouchable for the rest of their young lives. And while it is a popular past time for outsiders to blame the victims for all of their problems, who is to say that a powerless group doesn't have the right to make up its own definition of success, if the larger society doesn't include them in theirs.

Another form of negative reinforcement comes from the almost universal set of low expectations imposed upon Black youngsters and Black adults. We are branded inferior and incapable not only because we are Black, but also because we are from that crummy high school in the crummy neighborhood of Watts, the South Side of Chicago, North Philly, Newark, etc. Hundreds of thousands of Black folks have feelings of inferiority based on their Blackness, as well as on the degradation which has been allowed to flourish in the environments from which they come. Gangs, school systems, crime, dope and prostitution hangouts in relatively small communities have developed nationwide notoriety. And while some residents feel shame, many others consider it all part of the new perverse, inverted concept of success and fame. (They feel "everybody knows who we are").

As a result of ghetto life and low expectations there are basically three avenues a person can travel (as perceived by the ghetto resident):

a. You can participate in the perverted success game that is actively going on in the ghetto - play it until the law catches you in your life of crime. One could live quite well during that time proving once again that risk and reward are intimately related; OR

b. You can accept your "role" as a loser, chose not to even try to enter the larger society and live a fundamentally decent but poor life as a welfare recipient or semi-employed person; OR

c. You can enter the greater society taking special care to do only the safe and secure things. And just as you acted to avoid punishment as a child, here as an adult you act out of a *survival instinct*, a *"get over" philosophy*, where you avoid any challenge that would possibly reveal your perceived short comings.

A person entering the "real" world outside of the ghetto is often doing so without an intact self-concept or clear feeling of confidence and self-worth. Rather their self-perception is a big fat question mark. Who are they? Clearly, they are not the thugs of their neighborhood.. nor are they Sally or Fred sitting on the front steps for hours at a time, day after day surviving on unemployment or welfare checks. No they are not them, but they know and understand them. They often feel however, that they are much more like them than anybody else they know.

College, as was mentioned earlier, is supposed to be the transition station, where the human caterpillar is supposed to change into a beautiful butterfly after four years. Sometimes it happens, sometimes it doesn't. And sometimes it is unclear what went on in college accept a series of confusing experiences.

How does this relate to sales? Well as portrayed here the "typical" Black person's fear of failure is real and present. Even those who have gone to college, escaped the ghetto, and generally ignored the put downs, doubts, and low expectations given them by society's scriptwriters, are not at all sure who they are and what their capabilities are. Their self-confidence and self-concept is definitely vulnerable to sudden jarring motions and sharp prickly objects. And their personal working philosophy is likely to be "be cautious and survive." Is this the profile of a typical sales candidate? I would think not. A sales career means risk taking and daily rejections, and it rewards people financially only when they are successful and take the initiative. As stated earlier, most Blacks, as young people, never learn, or get a chance to get into the groove of being consistently rewarded for taking positive, aggressive action. How are you to develop this thing called initiative (self-directed action) when you have been told all of your life *to do what you are told*. Parents, baby sitters, teachers, the police and Army sergeants all take turns at telling young Black people what to do. To expect a young, Black adult to have initiative is like expecting a twenty-year worker of the night shift to become a "day" person or putting a car in reverse while going sixty down the highway and expecting nothing to happen to the transmission.

In short, selling is viewed by many Blacks, who are (were) brought up in the ghetto, not as a positive opportunity but as a shotgun with both barrels pointed at their heads. Out of the first barrel comes rejection on a daily basis, something they have had enough of to last the rest of their lives. Out of the other barrel comes insecurity in the form of inconsistent earnings in a field where success is everything and effort alone counts for almost nothing.

Learning to Deal With the Fear of Failure

Perhaps I should point out the obvious. I am not a psychologist or any kind of qualified person in the field of mental health. However, through study and personal experience, I have discovered some tips which seem to make sense and which have worked for those I know who have struggled with this thing called fear of failure.

The first step in dealing with the fear of failure is to admit to it and try to understand it. It is not just enough to read about the broad concept, you must try to understand how it affects you personally. I hope that what you have read in this section has given you some initial insight that you can build on as you see fit.

The second point to understand is that many people are successful *because of a fear of failure*. This might be somewhat puzzling so let me return to an earlier example. I had mentioned that some children were punished because they got low test scores and the result was that they developed a fear of tests and a fear of failing them. Failure led to what they feared the most - the punishment for getting poor grades. The truth of the matter is that this is not the only possible response to the situation. In millions of cases, because youngsters feared punishment, they put extra time and effort into studying their material so that they would be sure to do well on their exams and get great grades. This is precisely why their parents issued the threats in the first place. So many youngsters get good grades in this country *because* they fear failure. In other words, the fear of what will happen to them if they do fail is so great, they do things that assure them that they won't fail. This is referred to as acting *out of a fear of failure.* Some of the most accomplished and successful people in the country are so because they were motivated by threats and the fear of failure. To some people the feeling of shame is enough to make them work hard to prevent failure. It is called personal pride. These types of individuals do not need external threats of beatings or punishments because they are their own critics and they apply the pressure to themselves. Is this a good thing? Well, there is some debate on the issue. Some feel that the kind of personality who cannot tolerate losing is a candidate for heart attacks, strokes, ulcers, and a generally pressure-filled, worried state of mind. Others say it leads to crime and exploitation when a person will do anything and use anybody to win (or at least keep from losing). On the other hand, the self-starter, achievement oriented, goal setting personality has been held in such high esteem, particularly in the business world, that millions of people believe that the hate-to-lose, fear-of-failure personality is all part of the package and price of success. I leave you to make your own decision on this.

The next major concept to consider is that reality is often never as clear as it appears to be. Now this statement is not meant to introduce any sort of mystical, religious or spiritual thinking. The simple truth is that what is "obvious" to one person may not be "obvious" to another. For example, five different people have an interest in running. What is obvious to each one varies considerably.

I can run two miles; but "obviously" I can't run fifteen miles;

I can run fifteen miles but "obviously" a marathon (twenty six miles) is not possible for me;

I can run a marathon but "obviously" I need two strong legs to do it.

I can run a marathon and I only have one, good natural leg. "Obviously" I couldn't do it if that leg were taken from me.

I have no legs and I participated in and completed a marathon in my wheel chair. There are those who thought that was not possible. But it wasn't obvious to me so I did it.

Each one of the statements above is absolutely true and real to the person saying or thinking it. The truth is that it is not so much what happens to you in life as much as *how you respond to what happens to you* that makes all the difference in the world. About two months before I wrote this section there was a rash of teenage suicides. Most took their lives by sitting in a running automobile in a closed garage. I am willing to state unequivocally that the teenagers who took their lives during that time were not living under circumstances any more unbearable than those of other teenagers in this country. Yet for the pain and suffering they believed they were experiencing, death seemed to be a better answer. Thus the study of teenage suicide (or all suicide for that matter) is not so much a study of what happens to teens, but rather a study of why they *decide* to respond the way they do. There are tons of books on the market on positive thinking and related matters, and it is no accident that salespeople are one of the biggest users of these kinds of books. The point here is that people who wish to deal with their lifetime of negative reinforcement, lack of confidence and fear of failure can educate themselves to reinterpret the so called "obvious" reality that they deal with everyday.

The next point to understand in overcoming one's fear of failure is to appreciate the amount of learning that can take place by studying one's losses. Losing is not the *opposite* of winning, it is often just a step away from total victory. For example, suppose you were in a rifle shooting contest. After your first set of shots you examine your target and see that all your shots were off to the left. Next time you pull your gun to the right and shoot again. Result? You end up with several bull's eyes. Would it have made sense to quit after your first attempt? Of course not. In many instances in life, the line between winning and losing is a very fine one. To quit before a full commitment is made is to throw away all your previous lessons and efforts without any hope of a return. Quitting an activity can become habit forming. If you form the habit, it will cause you to lower the expectations you have of yourself and those that others have of you. If you have low expectations of yourself you will put out less effort and you will fail due to *lack of effort, not for lack of capability*.

To reduce the impact of losing you must learn to separate failing experiences *from each other*. You must dissect and study each situation individually. If you were to freely interrelate all of your losing efforts you would needlessly compound the power of all of them. You would make it easy to say to yourself, "I can't do anything right," and then quit. Black folks have special problems in this area.

Deep down in the consciousness of many Black folks there are many feelings of insecurity, doubt, inferiority and confusion relative to their ability to function within the broader White world. This insecurity and doubt is the result of the mental programing that Blacks receive on a daily basis. We absorb messages that remind us of a) our second class status because of our membership in the Black race, b) the disgust that people have for the communities we live in, and c) the low level of expectation and respect that people have for us as Black individuals. This constant flow of negative images and responses becomes like a permanent injury which remains sore, and is never allowed to heal. When some new problem, loss or failure hits us, it is very much like being hit on a body part that is already in pain. The pain we then feel is a *compounded* pain.

Sometimes it appears to be easy to blame our feelings of failure on the power of racism. We know that racism is real and the pain it causes is real. There are other times however, when we see our inadequacies in a very personal way, especially when it is clear that there is knowledge we lack, and there are skills we do not have. And then there are the in-between times when we don't know if our failures are the result of "the system", "bad luck", racism or ourselves. And because we often cannot find the true cause of some of our failures, we continue to fail repeatedly. We begin to expect problems and failures and when they occur they trigger memories of earlier failures and problems. A chain reaction begins and people are put into a state of depression.

Fighting the fear of failure requires that you stop associating problems that have nothing to do with one another. Many people (we are focusing on Black folks here) have a need to feel sorry for themselves. Actually, what they are really looking for are enough reasons, to justify to themselves, to quit the undertaking that they are engaged in. By lumping all of their pain, problems and failures together, they convince themselves that they are in a hopeless situation and therefore, they feel equipped to justify quitting to anyone that might inquire. It appears that Black people suffer this syndrome more than others. It appears that *we quit* more often than other people do. And as more Black folks see other Black folks quit time and time again, our fear that we too will fail and quit becomes even more real and more terrifying. We often begin operating our businesses out of a deeper and more tangible fear. Why is this the case? Why do we quit more? I have a few ideas, some of which have already been mentioned, that I would like to share with you.

First, we must all know by now that the barriers facing Black folks are more formidable and numerous. Our struggle for success then must be more intense; it requires more strength and endurance. It is easier to quit when there is the realization that you are simply not prepared for the magnitude of the struggle. Secondly, Blacks are not *expected* to be successful. Whites don't expect much from Blacks, and Blacks themselves don't expect each other to be very successful outside of our "traditional areas" (music, comedy, athletics, dancing, etc.). It is very hard for people to believe they can succeed if they are surrounded by people of all persuasions who share in the common belief that they will fail. The other alternative, almost as bad, is when Blacks are surrounded by people who do not care one way or another if they are successful or not.

The lack of expectation of success takes away a powerful incentive to succeed. For example, in many Asian communities we see people and families succeed because they fear bringing shame ("losing face") upon themselves and/or their families in the eyes of the community. They work extra hard because they are expected to succeed or suffer the emotional setbacks for failing to do so. In the underworld where criminal "families" or organizations exist, activity is very much guided by the expectations and codes of behavior that exist within that world. People who have the pressure of expectations placed upon them will usually work to meet those expectations. In fact the very essence of the word disappointment can be traced to not having met one's (or somebody else's) expectations.

Black folks, since they have noone who expects success from them, (at least in the world of business) have not been motivated by the type of pressure discussed here. They will embarrass, disappoint or "lose face" to noone because the expectations were never there. If, as many boast, people perform best when the pressure is on, then it also should stand to reason that many people underachieve due to the lack of pressure. Few things raise the pressure to perform more than one's peer group expecting him/her to win in a challenging situation.

Finally, I think most Black folks lack an appreciation for how much failure most successful businesspeople and salespeople experience before they eventually find success. Most Black success stories are about young people. We hear about young athletes, singers, actors, dancers and comedians. Many of these young people are succeeding in the first and only thing they have ever attempted. This gives rise to the impression that "you either have it or you don't." When people say what they want to be when they grow up, they usually mean at 21, 25 or 30 years old. The average businessperson doesn't even *begin* a *first* business until he/she is about thirty-two years old. And most successful businesspeople are not very successful in their first business. By the time they are rich and famous, they usually will have been in and out of half a dozen failing ventures. These failures, far more numerous than the successes, are almost never known to the public. If Colonel Harlan Saunders didn't start Kentucky Fried Chicken until he was sixty-five, what was he doing the first sixty-four years of his life?

In summary then I'm suggesting that you approach the fear of failing in several ways. In the first instance you can actually "use" the fear of failure to make the extra effort necessary to achieve your goal. It is a common reaction to this usually negative stimulus. Secondly, you can reinterpret your so called "handicaps." How you respond to your condition and its "reality" makes more of a difference than the actual condition itself in many cases. In the world of goal and achievement-oriented individuals, the line between the impossible and the possible is very blurry. Thirdly, you must learn what causes your failure(s). Usually, the more you understand what causes something, the less you generally fear it. You learn what causes your failure(s) by analyzing your mistakes. Your mistakes can be a source of tremendous enlightenment if you take the time to study them. Just by being clear within yourself about your shortcomings can make you proceed more confidently towards your goals. And sometimes just proceeding confidently may be just the thing to make you a winner. Lastly, you must separate your mistakes when you look at them and yourself. You do not allow your mistakes to be seen as a continuous avalanche burying you into the earth. Numerous mistakes just mean you have a lot of studying and learning to do. You must not quit, regardless of the number of your failures because you must perform up to your expectations. You must do this even if noone else is aware of the expectations you have of yourself.

You will also conquer your fear of failure by becoming more aware of the failures of other successful people. In essence you will learn to understand *the role of failure in developing success*. As you read about others you will understand that failure *is simply part of the dues* that virtually everyone has to pay on his/her way to the top.

The Trap You Don't Want To Fall Into

Reference was made earlier about how some poor Black folks develop different definitions of success because of a lack of access to real success and its benefits. I referred to it as perverted success, i.e., lavish wealth gained by selling dope to children, teen prostitution, etc. In this same Black world there exists a reversed sense of winning which also challenges common understanding. The simplest way to understand it I guess is to call it martyrdom. When people are convinced that the world is out to get them, and there is no way of winning in their minds, they sometimes reverse their tactics. Rather than avoid trouble they take pride in how much they can endure. This was the foundation of the civil rights movement. Do not fight back. Let them beat you in the head, sic dogs on you, throw you in jail, but don't fight back. The strategy is to let people see how strong you are, not based on what you can build or do, but on *how much you can take.* The more pain and misery you can take, the greater you are and the more respect people are supposed to develop for you. We see it in war where the heroes die, and we see it in boxing matches where we respect the loser for "being able to take all those punches and not go down." Undoubtedly there is a place for the endurance of pain and suffering. Certainly if our ancestors had not endured pain as slaves, we would not be here today.

But there is a danger for those people who, because they see no way of winning in the traditional ways, decide on a new tactic that often defies logic or common sense. I think that this is one of the fundamental ideas behind drug cultures. Often a person might say to him/herself, "you don't want me in your world, I'll leave it and live in my own, even if it leads to my destruction and death. I can deal with it."

Many depressed souls concoct ways to prove themselves all powerful and indestructible by simply absorbing all the power and destruction that is hurled their way. They have reversed their natural, mental processes in that rather than *fearing* failure, loss or pain they accept it as a challenge. You may keep a mental record of how much you have accomplished. They have a mental record of how much pain they have absorbed. One can see this distorted sense pride in homeless people who, in some instances, feel better about being able to survive in the elements than many people feel about the quality of their own homes. One can see why drugs and alcohol are such an important part of this lifestyle. The danger I see for the Black community is that the more people adopt this approach, the more others will tolerate it and even consider it for themselves if things get really bad. This perverted pride is a disease and like all diseases it can spread. The point is we must fight our fear of failure and like all fights it must be a fair one. We must fight our fear of failure by understanding what is going on within us and learn, lesson by lesson, from them. We must not "fight" failure by embracing it or learning to love it.

The Fear Of Success

Twenty-five years ago, in an atmosphere that was much more sexually conservative than today, teenagers used to ask each other "did you go all the way" after evenings with their dates. "Going all the way" referred, of course, to whether a couple actually made physical love or not during that particular evening. "Going all the way" was the specific goal of many young high schoolers (usually boys) while *not* going all the way was the primary objective of girls.

From the boy's point of view, sexual conquest was part of the definition of both masculinity and maturity no matter what other things you had going for you (intelligence, athletic ability, etc.) To be considered one of the guys, a real man, you had "to score." Young men usually feared failing this rite of passage because the ridicule could be maddening. But inside the hearts and minds of most of these young men was also the *fear of success*. There were the nagging questions of "what if." What if I score and she gets pregnant (which in those days meant she was definitely going to have a baby); that will ruin my life. What if I do it and I'm no good? What if she tells everybody that I'm no good? What if her parents or my parents find out?

From the girl's perspective, peer pressure to have sex in high school was rather mild in most places in 1962. Girls successfully avoided "going all the way" perhaps a majority of the time. But don't think for a minute, even in 1962, that there weren't some fears associated with successfully holding off persistent boyfriends. What if I lose him because I won't go to bed with him? What if other guys lose interest in me? What if they put me in the same bag as the other stuck-up prudes at school? What if I'm really missing this incredible feeling that everyone talks about?

I use the analogy above not because it directly relates to sales, but because it's important to understand that even as young people, we have had a problem defining and a fear of reaching the goals we set for ourselves. It is no wonder why, when confronted with success, we lose our confidence; it is a reminder of the confusions we had as youngsters.

It is unfortunate that Black Americans' lack of success in the business world is probably due more to a fear of success than to a fear of failure. I say this because fear of success is much less understood than fear of failure. Therefore, fear of success is one of those nagging problems that is never conquered because it is well hidden and ill-defined.

The Fear of Success in the Black Community

It is important, before I delve into the Black communities fear of success, that I try to define the concept. For the purposes of this book, I define the fear of success as a series of conflicting emotional and mental impressions and feelings. These feelings cause a person to stop, quit, drop out, back up, reverse, slow down or otherwise avoid the success that they previously sought and are capable of achieving. As you will see, fear of success used in this context is not actually *fear* as much as it is a concern about one's image as perceived by those of importance to him/her.

No community in the United States needs to experience "success" more than the Black community. Having been brought up to feel inferior, less intelligent, and dependent on the goodwill and power of Whites, Black folks need to continue their journey towards self-realization. This journey, which really accelerated during the civil rights movement, has slowed down because it has moved Black folks towards the economic arena and therefore, has been affected by their fear of success. Specifically, some of the concerns that many Black people have regarding the attainment of financial success are as follows:

a. GUILT: The unity that made for a successful Black movement was based around these themes: we are all in this together; in unity there is strength; united we stand, divided we fall, etc. The implication was that no person should seek to move faster than the movement of the group as a whole. The reality was that White America did not see Black folks as individuals, but as members of a despised group. Thus it was considered folly for a Black person to assume that he/she could be recognized as an individual. Today, 20 years later, there is much less unity and much more class structure and individualism in the Black community. While some Black folks could care less about the plight of those that they grew up with, others have a very different orientation. Many Blacks feel guilty because they have been allowed the opportunity to make money, live comfortable lives, be treated with respect and escape much of the hell of ghetto life, while many people they know with as much desire and ability, have been unable to do likewise. They question whether they *deserve* to live well when others, like themselves, are doing very poorly. As a result these individuals *do not* do all that they can to advance themselves because that would only bring on more guilt and discomfort. They slow down their efforts because they do not want their successes to widen the gulf between themselves and their less fortunate sisters and brothers.

b. ENVY: There is no analogy more frequently used when describing the mentality of Blacks than that of "crabs in the barrel." In essence, Black community members act like crabs in a barrel. As soon as one crab works its way to the top of the barrel, on the threshold of freedom, the other crabs pull this self-determined crab back into the barrel with them. Like it or not, this situation is a reality in the Black community in varying degrees. Successful Blacks are envied quite often. But unlike other communities where envy may serve to spur less-motivated individuals into action to achieve the same type of success achieved by "the role model", the Black community often allows envy to work in the reverse Successful people (the-would-be-role models), are sometimes the victims of hostility, jealousy and ostracism. The envy I'm referring to here sometimes builds into resentment. The Black community does not resent the economic success as much as the success-oriented attitude of the Black achiever. How dare a brother or sister act with boldness, confidence and assurance. The average Black person believes that his/her timid, conservative, risk-free approach to life is much more warranted given the circumstances of most Black folks. Rather than be inspired to greater heights by successful Blacks (and be expected to work harder and risk more in the process), poorer Blacks would rather see their own skeptical, lets-wait-and-see approach to life *confirmed*, by witnessing the downfall of a "cocky" achiever. Many Blacks do not want to see Black boldness rewarded because it would call for them to be bold and that is a pressure they do not want put upon them. They would rather see the bold crab fall back into the barrel.

All other times the "role model" is not a true success story because he/she has sold his/her soul to the other side. By this I mean that sometimes so called "Black success stories" are merely people who have tossed aside every aspect of their Black culture and background and taken on as many White mannerisms, values, and posturings as possible. From the Black communities point of view, what they are rejecting is not a "Black" role model but a manufactured White Negro who is an insult to the pride of the race. When you confuse White and Black definitions of success, legitimate indignation with pure jealousy and envy, ghetto perspectives with broader perspectives, you have one big mess. To avoid the potential hostility, envy and misinterpretation that could easily emerge from the Black community, many Black folks will simply draw the line as to how hard or how far they will push in their occupations and positions. It is not that they *fear* success, but they fear the *responses to their success of people they care about* .

c. *ALIENATION:* Alienation is a feeling that creeps up on people after a period of time, because they have emersed themselves in their own work world. Often times when successful Black people become so deeply involved in their work, they completely lose track of the time passed and how much of that time has been spent away from their families, neighbors and friends. Then, when a special occasion arises (a wedding, a funeral, a reunion and the like), the various differences between the hard-working achiever and regular people become obvious and dramatic. The successful person becomes aware of how little he/she has in common with former associates. They don't talk alike, or about the same topics. Their problems, as well as their successes, are vastly different. When asking each other "what's happening" the differences between their worlds become so obvious that each one is aware that the other is poorly pretending to be interested. This makes for a rather uncomfortable situation. Because success is harder to come by than mere survival, it is often the successful people who feel odd and out of place in group settings. They are the ones who feel alienated from the spirit of the group. When successful people experience these feelings, they are forced to ask themselves whether greater success is worth the greater alienation. The expression "it's lonely at the top" takes on a deeper meaning. What many seem to do, consciously or subconsciously, is to begin to slide back toward the group (at the expense of their work and future accomplishments) in order to feel more a part of it. They seek to be connected to something rather than be like an island sitting off by itself. Again, this is not a specific *fear* of success. It is, however, a possible outcome of success which, when experienced, slows down one's desire to reach out for more success.

d. *SEXUAL ALIENATION:* Among Black women sexual alienation is a real factor with regard to success. Already operating in an environment where they substantially outnumber eligible Black men, Black women have to determine how successful they want to be. Supposedly, women as a group, and Black women in particular, say that the more financially or professionally successful they are, the more intimidated men are about approaching them. In spite of the recent women's lib movement, many Black men and women are still more influenced by traditional roles and expectations than by any other factors. Thus, men expect women to "need them" and women expect to meet and date men who are doing "at least as well as they are." Therefore, the more successful a Black woman becomes, the more she is supposedly hurting her chances of finding a compatible Black man.

e. FEAR OF CHANGE: Very similar to and often confused with the fear of success is the general fear of change. Although many people will tell you that they do their best when the pressure is on, most individuals would rather live a life of understandable, predictable and controllable events than constantly have to respond to a lifestyle that is unpredictable and out of control. Almost everyone resists change, and those whose lives have a history of moving very slowly would probably be more likely to resist change than anyone else. Although a person's progress requires a change from what he/she is currently doing and experiencing, it also requires the responsibility of making new decisions. These decisions involve an element of risk which leaves one wide open for mistakes, failure and ridicule. Hence, some people cannot take advantage of an opportunity brought about by change because what they see are all the chances to make mistakes, take on more than they can handle, and perhaps, wind up no better off than before. The fear of change is what many people respond to in many conscious and subconscious ways. It has even been documented that people who have for years desired to lose weight, have, at the same time, undermined their weight loss efforts because they could not deal with the various changes that were beginning to take place in their lives.

Black-White Differences

Many of you who have just read the last few pages may very well be wondering whether the situations described above hold true for all people and not just Blacks. What is so special about the Black situation? The questions are fair and deserve a significant response.

First, as previously stated, the Black community needs success more than other communities. It currently suffers from the most poverty, drug abuse, unemployment, uncared for children, high school drops, homicides, plus many of the other negative things the world has to offer. If it is to turn around, the Black community must start to experience increased levels of success. And the momentum for success will not happen if the very individuals most ready to experience it decide not to "go for it", for the reasons outlined above. The White community is *filled* with successful people. Therefore, a successful White person is not as likely to feel as if he/she is deserting the White community because he/she never leaves it. He/she simply exchanges one kind of White community for another and consequently does not feel the degrees of guilt, envy, hostility, and alienation that Black folks experience. Given a preference, all people would probably appreciate relating to a peer group that shares similar viewpoints, experiences and interests. White people can find that in every city in America, though some cities, of course, are preferred over others. Successful Black people cannot assume that they will have the same options. Even in something as universally appreciated as professional sports, the situations differ. How is a star Black athlete supposed to feel "right at home" in Portland, Oregon; Phoenix, Arizona; or worse still, Green Bay, Wisconsin.

Another factor that makes for a difference between the White and Black experience is the degree to which Black Americans have adapted to (I use the term adopted rather than accepted) failure. If you are a fire-man, you get used to fire and heat, if you are a doctor you get use to blood, sickness and death. In the Black community, we learn to tolerate defeat and failure because that is our environment. Moreover, we actually begin to see, as a source of strength, the ability to withstand the pain and suffering in our community. The problem is not so much the fact that a few individuals take on this trait for psychic survival, but that the *whole race* adopts it for psychic survival. When you ask why Blacks settle for so little, you are challenging one of their survival mechanisms. When you question the Black community's ability to absorb defeat ("accept" defeat) you are questioning their institutionally-developed weapon against total self-destruction and madness.

The last difference between White and Black fears of success and failure that I will discuss revolves around Black success in the White context. When White people succeed in a White company there may very well be a certain amount of jealousy, envy, hostility and negativity.

But there are often compensating responses as well. A successful White may be portrayed as a role model. There may be a promotion involved as well as the respect from colleagues and peers. A successful White may even be asked to share the secrets of his/her success with the rest of the team.

A Black person's success in a White context may be received quite differently. In addition to being concerned about the responses of and interrelationships with his/her community, a Black person may also have to deal with the White community's response to his/her success in the workplace. When Blacks are successful on the job, particularly in sales, they do not become role models. White people seldom seek to copy Black folks' ways of doing anything (except in music and dance). Blacks are not held out as examples such that sales managers say "all of you should be more like him/her." Instead of being asked for their secrets of success, their Blackness *intensifies* the normal jealousy and hostility they would feel if they were White. It is not only more intense, but also it more than likely would come from many more people. Since neither White nor Black people *expect* success from Black folks, when they do achieve it, they get demeaning responses. It is either due to luck, "natural" talent, reverse discrimination, affirmative-action quotas or some other discounted reason. Seldom is it attributed to hard work, brilliance, persistence or other more complimentary reasons for success.

There is a general feeling among millions of Whites that Blacks should be humble and thankful for what they have in America and shouldn't be greedy for more. Unfortunately, they have communicated this mindset so well that too many Blacks have embraced it as their own feeling as well. It is another reason why Blacks avoid success and the limelight.

Fear of Success as it Relates to Selling

Many aspects of the fear of success have been discussed thus far and it should be easy to see how they may affect Black folks' attitudes towards selling. We are a people who do not yet live in the totality of

America, but mostly in pockets of Black communities in about forty metropolitan areas. In our communities, it is not uncommon for everybody to know everybody else. As a result, we take care to protect our images among those we feel destined to be around for the majority of our lives. The fear of success, as explained, seems to be more a concern about image than actual, emotional fear of being successful.

Guilt may very well enter the mind of a successful salesperson who knows that his/her job is a breeze compared to the dirty, dangerous, low-paying, physically-demanding work that his/her friends are doing. This guilt could be subconscious until a horror story about bad treatment, loss of job, injury or loss of life surfaces regarding a friend or acquaintance. There is often guilt in just being associated with certain White companies because their image becomes the salesperson's image and many times the two are mismatched.

Is there envy and hostility directed toward Blacks who are successful salespeople? Probably no more than that directed toward other successful people. The White community, believing that success is their birthright, is more likely to express hostility and jealously toward Black associates who experience selling and income success. Few things make a White American feel as inadequate as failing to do as well as a Black person in something that they consider "their" specialty. Their feelings are expressed overtly or through back-stabbing, behind-the-scenes actions. One can understand why most Blacks would be cautious about "going for broke" and why they back away from reaching their maximum potential in these White environments.

Alienation, however, is something that a Black salesperson is more likely to feel since it is probably caused by not fitting into either community. Once a salesperson really gets into the mental framework of selling, risking, losing, profiting, budgeting, maneuvering, etc., it becomes more difficult to relate to fellow Blacks who complain about not having a high paying job fall into their laps. When, as a salesperson, you learn how to turn a "no" into a "yes" everyday, you lose patience with people who complain about their jobs and who have no intention of doing anything about it. In other words, a successful Black salesperson loses the ability to empathize with the Black underdog because he/she is aware of how much opportunity there is in the country and how much of it could belong to other Blacks if they just went for it. On the other hand, Black salespeople realize that they will never be White and therefore have very little chance to become a part of the "good ole boy network" that runs the major companies in this country. Regardless of how much Black people philosophically buy into the so called "capitalistic way of thinking" and the "dress for success syndrome", they are still recognized as Black first and therefore ineligible for membership into any other family but their own. This adds to the fear of success because as Blacks become more successful at selling to White America, they know that they are becoming more dependent on consistent, positive responses from Whites to maintain their lifestyles. This need to stay on the "good side" of clients causes many Blacks to compromise their principles and values, and nobody is more aware of this than the Black salesperson. The greater the success and upward mobility the greater the fear of compromise.

The other fear that probably haunts all salespeople, but is more likely to bother Blacks, is the fear of failing after being successful. First of all, you must understand that many Blacks feel that we have no business in sales because it is not perceived as relevant or uplifting work for the Black community's interests. So when a person enters the sales profession and becomes successful there is often little celebration in the Black community. The attitude is often, "Yeah they may be flying high right now, but they'll come crashing down to reality soon enough and get a regular paying job like they have some sense." Unfortunately, many Blacks, for whatever reason, do leave sales positions discouraged and return to salaried work. This is in the back of the minds of virtually all Black salespeople. They fear the experience of climbing the mountain, and beating their chest only to slip and fall all the way back down into the valley among people who are ready to ridicule and chastise.

Overcoming the Fear of Success

The first step in overcoming the fear of success is understanding exactly what it is. I have shared some viewpoints with you here, but you must delve deeper into your own personality, environment and motivations to see what specifically makes you tick. It might help to write down your concerns and reflect on them. In so doing, you have to decide just how much you are going to allow what others think of you control what you will and will not attempt to do. I believe that we Black folks have to be clear in deciding whether we are interested primarily in love, or respect from each other and the outer world. Of course, it would always be nice to have both, but we often have to make choices.

The next step is to accept change as a condition of life and not fear it. Success is rapid movement and change in a positive direction. So you have to not only accept change, but also promote and embrace it if success is really what you want. And with success comes pressure and higher expectations because you cannot consistently improve something and have it become known to people without those same people *learning* to expect improvement and consistency from you. Successful people go through cycles of creating expectations in others and themselves, and then they go about fulfilling them.

The third aspect of fighting the fear of success is developing confidence. Confidence is not a 'know it all' attitude. Confidence means feeling good enough about one's ability to make good judgements so as not to fear new or strange situations. Confident people believe, that when confronted by a situation that is out of their control, they will eventually make the decision that is in their best interest. And, they believe that if they make a bad decision they can regroup and make a second decision that is better than the first. But it is difficult to do this if you really don't know what you want in the first place.

Flexibility is a new demand that has been placed on all people who are the movers and shakers of the world. At one time the U.S. did not care what the Japanese or the Arab world thought about anything. Today, this is not the case. It seems that today, people are used to playing different roles, showing different faces, wearing different hats and speaking different languages in order to get their points and purposes across. Then in the comfort of their own homes, after having obtained from the larger world what they wanted, they can be and do what they wish. This, I think, is what is very necessary for Black folks to do, especially in sales. We have to learn how to realistically play roles in order to get what we want. Do you think America's newest immigrants from Asia, the Middle East, Cuba and South America act, speak and dress in public exactly the way they do in their own homes and communities? I don't think so. Black Americans really don't have to give up being Black when they work for White sales companies. They merely have to know when to turn on and off their role-playing button when entering and leaving the two communities. Black folks' problem, unlike other folks' problem, is confusion over just what their identity is. What Blackness is, and whether it is something to love and be proud of or hate and run away from, has been the single, biggest issue in our community for the last twenty-five years. It is hard for people to think that they can be clear about their professional identities when they are still confused about their social and cultural identities. Once we, as individuals and as a people, are clear about who we are, we will be able to switch roles and gears along with the rest of the international community and accept changes and successes as they come our way.

Supporting Black institutions is something that all Black folks should do, but it is even more important for Black salespeople to do. We know that Black salespeople help White companies make more money and we know that as successful salespeople Blacks make a good deal of money for themselves. The obvious expectation then is that salespeople use part of their earned wealth to enrich the community from which they emerged, even if they no longer live there. Black organizations, churches, colleges, charities and other causes are always in need of funds. There are plenty of non-profits to go around to everybody. Nothing kills guilt like making a handsome contribution to a worthy cause; similarly, nothing improves the image of the so-called "greedy" salesperson than having the community see him/her make a contribution. It should be mentioned, of course, that there are many more ways to help the Black community than just giving money. But if money is your biggest asset and the community's biggest need, why not make that the priority.

The final thing that I will suggest in dealing with the fear of success and relationships with people is that we have to get away from the idea that Black folks are one homogeneous group. Because we have been brought up under some sick and sad circumstances, there are people who are reflective of their environment; sick and sad. People will curse you, be jealous of you and try to harm you whether you're successful or not. If you cannot learn to accept that, then perhaps sales is not the field for you. Salespeople *try* to please their customers all the time, their livelihoods depend on it. But all salespeople know that they cannot please all of their clients, much less everyone else, all the time and they accept that as the reality.

PREPARING FOR
SUCCESS IN SALES

If you are still reading up to this point you must be strongly leaning towards a career in sales, or at least considering it. And by now, several things should be clear to you. You should clearly understand why sales is an area of business that Black folks should definitely begin to master and why it answers some of our problems and offers us distinct opportunities. You should be aware of why we as a people, are just now beginning to look at sales, as a career option. Finally, since I have examined the twin fears of failure and success, you should also be able to see how these two pressures more intensely affect the Black community than the general population. Assuming that you, in fact, understand these things, I will now proceed with the actual "how to" aspects of selling.

Definition of Sales

It would make sense at this point to define what is meant by the term sales or selling. There are a lot of misconceptions about what selling is and even though I have used the term many times thus far, it has not yet been defined. It serves no purpose, that I am aware of, to give just one definition of selling. It might be easier if there were a single, universally accepted concept, but I have not found one. So, I offer multiple definitions, all of which fit a number of situations.

Selling Is:
 a. Transferring a person's beliefs and convictions about a product or service to another person in such a way that the latter not only feels the same way as the salesperson, but actually buys the product as a result.
 b. Asking a person a number of specific questions so as to lead to

a purchase that is in his/her best interest.

c. Helping a person make a decision that is difficult, yet ultimately turns out to be a good one.

d. Helping a person make a *new* decision (by giving new and additional information) when his/her mind seems to be set on something else.

There are countless definitions of selling, and what it is in one situation will not be what it is in another, even though the same product and salesperson may be involved. One of the goals of this book, in fact, is to expose you to enough information about sales so that you will be able, over time, to develop your own definition(s) and philosophy(ies) about it.

Ways of Selling

One of the chief reasons why many people back away from selling is because they assume there is only one way to do it. Selling, in their minds, is talking to strangers, *face to face,* all the time and pretending to care when they don't even know them. To many, it is counting on their ability to win peoples' confidence so that they will give up twenty, a hundred or a thousand dollars after a five-minute conversation. It is no wonder with this limited view of selling, so many people run for cover at the very mention of the word. Fortunately, this perception is just that - a perception. Selling is so broad in scope it allows for a number of ways to attract dollars from consumers.

1. Direct Sales

The most fundamental method of selling is the direct approach. Millions of salespeople do, in fact, talk to strangers every day in order to explain the products they offer in the hopes of making a sale(s). Usually these meetings take place in stores or businesses. This is where selling started, and in many places it is where the final sale is made after initial contact through other means. Although one shouldn't assume that he/she will always have to face and sell to strangers directly, it should not be a situation that one avoids.

2. *Mail-Order or Catalogue Sales.*

Because the U.S. is such a large country, there are often tremendous distances between companies with a product to sell and a customer who wants to buy it. Over a hundred years ago, this problem was addressed when some companies decided to print pictures of its products in a book, and use the postal system to get the merchandise to and money from its customers. Today the single word to describe this form of selling is mail-order. There are millions of catalogues produced and mailed to millions of people. Millions of products are sold and shipped and millions of dollars are collected which leads to millions of dollars in profits. If you are absolutely certain that you could never talk to customers face-to-face, then mail-order may be a part of your future.

3. *Telemarketing*

Telemarketing is about as old as the telephone itself. It is probably the half-way point between direct selling and mail-order selling. You do talk to people, but not face-to-face. And very often, the distances between company and customer is as great as any distance the mail might travel. A person's ability to effectively communicate is very important in telemarketing, as well as, certain skills that may not be as strongly required in other areas of sales.

4. *Wholesaling*

Virtually every item sold in this country travels through a network of temporary destinations before it reaches the final consumer. Often this network includes a warehouse where products are stored after they leave the factory, but before they get to the retail store. People who own or work in warehouses often sell large quantities of goods to retailers.

There are people who don't mind selling as a process, but simply tire of individual customers saying, "I don't have the money". These people may find some relief in wholesaling because in this field, other businesses, not individuals, are the clients and they *have to buy* in order to stay in business. They must buy from a wholesaler in order to sell to everybody else. Although wholesaling is often a low profit-margin business with feast and famine periods of activity, it's worth investigating.

5. Corporate Selling

Corporate selling shares many of the characteristics of other areas of sales. Like wholesaling, you sell to companies, not individuals per se, and you do talk to strangers (as in direct sales) until they become regular clients. Often the sale can be completed over the telephone. The products purchased and the money collected usually involve people other than those making the initial transaction. American corporations spend an astronomical amount of money on goods and services - from skyscrapers to paper clips and everything in between. It is an area where Black folks have increased their representation in the last ten years and one of growing opportunities. The requirements for participation in this area of sales, however, are usually more rigid than in any other.

6. Multi-Level Sales

This method of selling is a form of direct sales and actually requires two distinct, but related skills. One must be prepared to sell a product face-to-face as well as to train other individuals to sell the product. A good multi-level salesperson must teach those immediately reporting to him/her how to train a third tier of salespeople in order to form a viable and lucrative sales network.

There are other types of sales that are available for people to consider. The purpose here is not to give an exhaustive listing, but to convince a novice that he/she should not assume that all selling is the same and that it does not always involve a continuous interaction with strangers.

How Do You Get Paid In Sales?

The bottom line is the bottom line right? People work for many reasons and money is always at or near the top of the list. I have said that some people dislike risk, generally speaking, and prefer stability and steady pay. I have suggested that selling is different. The truth of the matter is that it can be different and it usually is different but it isn't always different. Confused? Good, now you will pay attention so you can become unconfused.

a.   Straight Salary: One of the most common mistakes people make is to call a salesclerk a salesman or saleswoman. This mistake is understandable, partly because one of the distinguishing features between the two is how they get paid. And since customers seldom know how a person gets paid, it's all the same to them anyway. For clarity's sake, a salesclerk is usually someone who gets a straight salary (probably starting at minimum wage) and basically takes orders. For example, if you walk into McDonald's and ask for a Big Mac, large Coke and small fries, the person to whom you speak is a *salesclerk*. He/she isn't selling you anything, just taking your order. You would order the same thing no matter who you were speaking to and you aren't interested in his/her opinion on what you should eat. Furthermore, the person who takes your order will get paid the same salary whether you order or not. Whether salesclerks take a hundred orders a day or a hundred and four they will still receive the same wage. There is no relationship between the amount of money that passes through salesclerks' hands and the amount of money they are paid. In most cases, this is not the way it is for real salespeople.

b.   Salary Plus Commission: An employee receives a regular salary upon which he/she can depend. This salary will be received on a continuous basis unless the employee is not selling the minimum dollar amount necessary to remain employed. An employer, of course, wants "good" people, and a good salesperson is one who can make a lot of sales. Storeowners like to hire salespeople who can persuade a customer to spend one hundred dollars when he/she only intended to spend fifty. In order for owners to get employees who are capable of this, they have to pay. So they will pay a percentage of all sales over a specified minimum to the salesperson responsible for those sales. This incentive gives salespeople the chance to make more than their normal salary, and it allows the storeowner to get people to do all the extra things that make a business successful. Both parties, therefore, are winners. Additionally, the customer wins because rather than being met by a tired unenthusiastic, robot-like creature asking "Can I have your order?", he/she is served by an enthusiastic human being who has something to gain by being pleasant and helpful. So, a second way of getting paid in the sales field is by salary and commission. An example of this method of payment can be seen in shoe sales where there is a direct relationship between the number of shoes sold and the dollars earned over and above the salary paid.

c.   Salary Draw and Commission: Suppose you've landed a job selling typewriters to businesses in your city. The position required a college education, two or three types of tests and several interviews. Chances are you're offered some type of salary right? Right. Does that make you a salesclerk? No. You have to go out and drum up customers after the proper amount of training. And chances are that even after your training period, you will not experience selling success for at least six months to a year. So companies that sell to other companies and that want top notch salespeople to do the selling, will offer a salary called a draw. What this means is that a company will pay you a salary with the expectation that you will earn the money back once sales start to pick up. They are really taking a chance by not only paying and training you, but by paying the other costs associated with making a sale (travel, promotional materials, sales literature, etc.) As you earn commissions, you and your employer settle your account (i.e. you pay back your "loan"). Eventually the draw salary gets smaller which means two things: a) you owe your employer less money, and, b) you should be making regular sales since you will need the commission to augment the reduced income your employer is lending you. Often in salary draw situations the draw is not a loan but a real "temporary" salary to keep you going until you learn how to sell your product. In most instances, a salesperson is expected to graduate from a "draw" position to a full commission income.

d.   Full Commission: "Real" salespeople live or die based on how well they sell. Would you rank doctors based on their grades in medical school or how well they helped their patients. Would you pay a professional athlete based on newspaper clippings from college or how well he/she helped the team win.

In sales, it is usually the case that those who sell well get paid well and those who don't can go home. One of the major reasons why there are so many people in this country with real estate licenses who are no longer selling is because real estate is an all or nothing business. Thousands of people have gone for months with absolutely no income and then in one month have made thousands of dollars from a single sale. In real estate, especially if there is no savings account or backup support system, the goal is to sell a house before one starves. Not only can this be stressful on one's home/personal life, but also understand that each potential client must not be even vaguely aware that the salesperson hasn't sold a piece of property in months. After all, what would someone think of the salesperson if this were known?

Why do people go for "commission only" positions when they can get "salary plus commission" positions you may be asking? It's all due to the bottom line? Why do people play football, drive race cars or clean windows from the 78th floor? Two reasons: because it pays well and because of what they think *they* can do as opposed to someone else.

The commissions paid in salary plus commission positions are small, and generally speaking, there are limitations. For example, there are only so many people that will enter a shoe store during a given time period. This does not mean, however, that one cannot earn a good income. But there is a law in business that applies most of the time that says, the greater the risk the greater the return. In commission only sales positions the commissions are high (either in absolute dollars or in percentages) and usually the wealthiest salespeople are in these types of positions.

e.   Sales Territory - Sales Management: Because there are limits to what any one person can do and since a good person is hard to find, businesses have come up with ways to help people make more money through their sales experience. Often this is achieved by giving people a sales territory or management responsibility. In this case, someone who has demonstrated sales savvy is given the task of managing other people and/or a geographic area. The belief is that the manager can provide expertise in training, motivating or supervising other people. The reward is a commission or percentage of all the sales generated in that region or among those salespeople under the manager's supervision. Thus, the commission check increases because it is derived from the efforts of several or many people rather than from one person. Sometimes a sales manager will make additional commissions by servicing long-term clients. Consequently, there are instances where a person not only receives more commission money but possibly a double commission as well.

f.   Percentage of Profits - Year End Bonus: Many companies allow top salespeople to share in the year-end profits. For the company there are several advantages. First, by waiting until the end of the year, a company can be sure that there is a profit before handing out goodies to everyone. Secondly, the company can plan an income tax strategy - it can keep or give away profits which will definitely impact the tax obligation. Finally, poorly performing salespeople are motivated to set New Year resolutions and particularly goals, when they see how much income their fellow co-workers earned. For employees, year-end bonuses come at a time when they do a great deal of spending (Christmas, Kwanzaa, etc.) and since the money comes in a big chunk they can make a major move in their financial lives (buy property, pay college tuition, buy stocks, etc.)

These are just a few of the ways salespeople are paid. It should also be pointed out that millions of salespeople have multiple pay periods. As a salaried employee, you usually get paid twice in most months. Often financial troubles stem not from how *much* you get paid, but how frequently (or infrequently if you prefer) you get paid. Salespeople may get three, five or ten pay checks at various times during a month. For people with a good mail-order business, pay day can be just about every day of the year. Wouldn't it be nice to get more money more often. Commission sales is this way.

Changes in Lifestyle and Workstyle

When people elect to become involved in sales, they not only have to prepare for more risk in their lives, they often have to rearrange their lives completely. Answer this question, When are goods and services sold in this country? If you said every second of every minute of every day, then you are right. That's why there is so much opportunity to make money because there are so many things to sell and so many people to buy them. Because sales activity is constant, the salesperson is constantly active. As a matter of fact, while many people are relaxing, salespeople, if they are dedicated, are working their hardest. Ever see a mall on the weekends or just before Christmas? While many employees are going to various office parties, during and after work, between December 15th and January 3rd, many salespeople are putting in sixteen hour days. The same can be said for other holidays. Does this affect family life? Think about it for a few minutes. What about travel? In most nine-to-five jobs, people are home for dinner just about every night. However, many salespeople must spend up to half of each year on the road to earn the income that their families enjoy back home. They are by no means unique, since athletes, actors, politicians, musicians and other performers and celebrities must do the same. I bring this up to point out yet another price to be paid to earn the type of wealth that is available to salespeople.

In addition to the irregular working hours involved in sales, it is important to be aware of the need for budgeting. In theory, we all budget our expenses and income so that there is some kind of match. In a salary situation, we know exactly how much money we will have and when we will receive it. Such is not the case in sales. One must always have some form of cash reserve because there will inevitably be periods when sales and income slow down. This means that salespeople have to be disciplined in their spending. And like all disciplined activity it is not much fun for the worker-consumer. Most people are convinced that they won't earn enough to make ends meet. To ask a person who thinks this way to save a significant portion of this already "small" income is asking alot. In sales it is a must. If you fail to save and budget, you will inevitably give yourself enough excuses and reasons to quit and go back to a salaried job. You will blame your product line, your company, your commission fees and a host of other things, but you will not blame yourself for failing to maintain a budget and keep something in reserve.

Identifying Yourself With A Product

If you believe that you're ready to endure the discipline and sacrifices needed to reap the benefits of selling, then you have a very important decision to make. The decision that will determine your success in sales, perhaps more than any other is the type of product you will sell. To talk about selling without selecting a product is like training for the Olympics without deciding what sporting events you are preparing for. Although there are many similarities in the selling process regardless of the product being sold, (just as running, weight lifting and stretching can be part of the training for a number of sports) the key aspect of the selling process is *believabilty*. Do you believe in the product? Can you communicate this belief to your customers? Can they believe in you and the product after you have communicated your ideas. The product that you select is key because you must believe in it first before you can communicate that belief to *your* customers. Anything less will come off as a possible con job and even an unsophisticated person will be skeptical. Many times people will jump into a sales position and push something that is "hot" or a current fad. They expect the product to take off and sell itself without much effort on their part. Usually it doesn't work. Sometimes a fad will unexplainably take off, especially if the media picks up on it. But in almost all instances, people who value their money will buy things for emotional and rational reasons. The salesperson is more believable if he/she shares the same or similar emotions and reasons as the client.

Many people have trouble choosing a product to sell. It is not an easy decision to make because there are a number of things to take into consideration. But I believe that the key an instinctive identification with a product or service. In your life time you have seen a coat, a suit, a car, a painting or something and said "Now this is me." Something about the item struck you in such a way that you didn't merely say *I like it,* instead you totally identified with the product and said *it was you.* I believe that some kind of identification must exist with the product one is to sell. I believe it should be so strong that you almost see the product as a symbolic extension of your personality. You will probably find that it is easier to feel this way about a service you provide than an actual product made in South Korea or somewhere else. Fortunately, you live in a country where everything is for sale. One merely has to select a product and then prepare oneself to sell it. What turns you on: clothes, cars, houses, food, music or paintings? Whatever turns you on: can be sold to the market that buys these kinds of things. What does this mean to you? It means you need to have a very good idea of yourself before you can really be successful in sales.

Many people entering the sales field hop from product to product in an effort to see what works. But their foundation is weak because they really don't know themselves. They don't need to find out how products work, they need to find out how *they* work. Just because they get involved in sales doesn't mean that they give up the idea of defining their role and purpose in life. Just as a doctor's mission is to heal the sick, a lawyer's mission is to defend the innocent and a politician's mission is to serve the public, a salesperson believes his/her only mission is to sell and make money. While I'm sure some people believe this, I do not. As a matter of fact, I find that the best salespeople have a sense of a mission that's directly tied to the product they sell. A real estate salesperson, for instance, may believe that his/her mission in life is to help people move into the best environment that they can afford. An insurance salesperson should believe in giving people a sense of protection and security. A computer salesperson may believe that he/she is the key to helping companies increase efficiency.

So I'll repeat what has been stated already. The single greatest decision necessary for your sales success is determining what you want to sell and the key to that decision is knowledge of yourself. You need to know what you like; but you also need to try to link what you like with a purpose in life. Is this easy? No not really. It is usually a process that evolves over a period of time. Many salespeople start out with a product and overtime learn what they like and dislike about selling it. If they find they don't like it, they may switch to a product or service for which they are better suited. The important thing, however, is to make money while this analysis is going on. Poverty leads to desperation and rarely are good lasting decisions made during periods of stress and desperation.

After selecting a product to sell, a salesperson must then identify the market. Who is going to buy that product and why should it be purchased from that salesperson as opposed to someone else? This is especially a concern when Blacks enter a field new to them. Is it likely that Whites or Blacks will run to support a new Black salesperson who looks almost out of place to the casual observer? NO, it is not likely. But in this particular part of Black-American history, it is up to this generation to begin a tradition of sales in areas that have been uncharted by Blacks. This is called opportunity. This is called having new options. Fortunately the company you work for or represent will have plenty of information on prospective clients. If you feel good about your product it will come across and eventually you will succeed, especially if you become an expert, not only in selling techniques, but also on the industry into which your product or service fits. Is this a lot to ask of an individual? Yes it is. But it is easier than curing AIDS, stopping teenage pregnancy or housing the homeless. And you are going to earn more money than most of the people tackling those problems.

It is probably in your best interest to begin selling on a part-time basis. Most things can be sold this way. You may not be able to work for the best companies or sell the newest and best products part-time, but you can at least enter the field and feel your way around to determine whether the product and market is right for you.

Sales Motivation

In many job situations one can often just go through the motions of work while allowing the mind to wonder. Postal workers do it, cooks do it, virtually everyone does it. But it is difficult to do your job in sales and think about something other than the job at hand. Every customer is a unique challenge and opportunity. Every customer wants: personalized attention, questions answered, and to believe what he/she is being told. Salespeople have to be properly motivated in order to interact effectively with clients. It is unrealistic to expect people to always be *"up"* no matter how much they love their product or company. Realistically, salespeople must be able to draw on some source of inspiration, encouragement and enthusiasm. Failure to develop some type of motivational system could lead to poor performance and income for those going through down cycles.

It's particularly important that Black salespeople develop a motivational system for at least three reasons. First, as this is the beginning era of Black involvement in sales, there are doubts, both in the minds of salespeople and the companies they represent, as to whether they are capable of selling. They need to prove to everyone's satisfaction that Blacks are capable of selling everything on the market. Secondly, the motivational systems designed by the companies they represent are often corny at best (except for the financial incentives); corny songs and cheers, company parties and rallies, and role models. If that system doesn't turn them on, they can't ignore the fact that they have to develop their own because they *will* have moments when their faith, confidence and values begin to slip below acceptable levels. Finally, they need a motivational system because our people need a system. What do I mean by this? Well right now, there is a hopelessness that pervades entire communities and there are very few real institutions or leaders that have the ability to change its general mood. Depression over drugs, housing, education, Black-on-Black crime, the working poor, the homeless, AIDS, teenage pregnancy and a host of other problems sap the motivation and enthusiasm from millions of Blacks who have so little to believe in anyway. In the past, the hopes of Black people rested on the achievement of concrete objectives. We eliminated segregation in part, we won the right to vote, we elected Black mayors and we stopped the War in Vietnam. With all of these accomplishments behind us there are many who say that things are worse than ever and that there is a permanent underclass in the community that will never make it. In the past we had leaders who seemed to pave the way to a greater future. Martin Luther King Jr., the Honorable Elijah Muhammad, Stokley Carmichael and others. It was impossible for an upcoming Muhammad Ali fight not to pull the community out of its doldrums and swell the hearts of millions with deeply felt pride for at least week or so. But today everything is pretty much taken for granted. Even for a Black man to be running as a serious presidential candidate is no big deal today. So what do some Blacks say? They say, "What's in it for me?, he can't win anyway so why *waste a* vote."

What does all this have to do with Black salespeople developing a motivational system? Well, in my opinion, there is a connection. You see if you study Black history you will notice that our advancement comes in surges, not as one continuous motion. And, if you look back, you will see that within the Movement there was always a *certain sector* of the

Black community who served as the leading advocates for change, and whose actions affected most areas of Black-American life. For example, during World War II, Black soldiers stood on the front lines of change. Their idea was to fight for the U.S. abroad, and refuse to accept and fight against segregation and second classness as a way of life when they got home. In the early fifties, the legal community of the NAACP stood out front. Armed with Black scholars, research and the law, they pushed down the legal walls that blocked our progress. In the early sixties, Black college students took their turn, through sit ins, freedom rides, marches, etc., and their impact was felt. From the mid-sixties to 1970, the so-called hoodlum or extremist brother got into the act. By burning down parts of cities, intimidating the police and challenging the powers that be, a very strong statement was made to America. From the early seventies to the present there has been relatively little action going on in our communities; maybe the symbolic election of a Black politician on occasion. I believe it is up to the new entrepreneurial class to be today's new warriors. Today it's about information and money control. The Black salesperson has to be part of the systematic shake-up of the relationship between Black people and money. We have shaken up the political, military, and higher educational system, now we need to shake-up the economic system.

Black salespeople have to learn to motivate themselves not just for their own success (financially and otherwise), but also to be a part of a nationwide *movement* by Blacks to capture a part of the money supply. They must see themselves as the single most important group in the Black community at this time. They must see that they are about the only group that can demonstrate something *new* to the Black community. And, they must see that one of the major reasons why they are so important is because what they are doing can be duplicated by thousands of others. Only a few can become doctors, lawyers, mayors or major movie or rock stars. But thousands upon thousands can become successful sales and business people. And what better time to do it than now, when we are running many of America's major cities (who knows how long this will last).

I would like for you to note two things as you look at history and our future challenges. Hopefully, these two ideas will affect your way of thinking about Black America's tasks of today. The first thing I want you to look at is the pattern of war between the U.S. and its enemies in the last forty-five years. In World War II, the U.S. fought Germany and Hitler, Italy and Mussolini, but it was the bombing of Pearl Harbor by *Japan* that actually got us into the war. Later we fought North Korea for a few years and then came the very long war with Vietnam which involved China, Laos, Thailand and other Asian nations. In the past forty-five years, this nation's enemy has consistently been Asian people. Now ask yourself with whom does this country do an increasing amount of business. You got it, those same Asian people: Japanese, Koreans, Filipinos, Taiwanese, Vietnamese and others. Not only does this country do business with them internationally, but it welcomes, accepts and admires them when they come to this country and become successful. I raise this point because the Black American's struggle for freedom has seemingly been about *White Love*. We wanted Whites to love us, teach us, let us sit by them, let us vote for them, let us work for them, let us take care of their children and clean their houses - just love us. Yet what seems to be stronger than love is *respect*. I do not believe the typical American loves Asians any more today than they did ten short years ago. Movies are still being made about the trauma Americans went through trying to kill them. But what *has* emerged since those wars is a *respect* for Asians. This *respect* allows them to do business together. This *respect* allows them to accept each other's word. Enemies who have *respect* seem to get better treatment from White Americans than do Black Americans who seem to be willing to do anything for love. We need to change! The old stuff is old stuff. We need *respect*. Seek ye *respect* and all other things should pretty much come to thee. And what gains respect not only in America, but also in the world is information and money. If you have information and no money that breeds *disrespect* because people will wonder, "If you're so smart, why aren't you rich? Something must be wrong with you." And if you can gain respect throughout the rest of the world for having information and money, then you will get more respect at home because everyone is compelled to recognize someone who is internationally recognized. Muhammad Ali is one of the best examples of this.

The second thing I would like for you to do is to compare our last "great movement" (Civil Rights 1960-69) with our challenges of today. In the 60's we took on the struggle with very little resources. We had very little money or organization, few prepared leaders, and plenty of negativism, apathy and internal dissension. Yet Black Americans largely prevailed. What were our weapons or tools for the job? We had our mouths (for singing, protesting, demanding and encouraging), our beliefs (in our hearts we knew it was the right thing to do and We *Shall* Overcome - deep in our hearts we do believe that we shall overcome some day) and our feet (for marching hundreds and thousands of miles). We also had our *guts;* we faced the Ku Klux Klan, police and sheriffs, mobs, dogs, bombs, guns, jail and death itself, yet we kept moving. That is our history. As we look at the challenge facing us in sales and business, what do we really need to succeed? To sell you need: your mouth (to make presentations, respond to objections and ask for the money) and your feet (to go out and find the people, march hundreds of miles if you have to). The question is, Do we have the other two things needed for sales success? Whether we have the belief (virtually every immigrant group in the history of America has sold its way to success, can we? Can we make money like everybody else or will we need "special programs", "quotas" and "set asides" for the rest of the history of the universe) and the guts is questionable. Which is harder, facing the Klan or facing White America and asking for an order. Think about it.

In recapping this section on motivation, there are a few things I'd like to reiterate. Black salespeople must develop a way to motivate themselves because sales success will not happen if they continue to go through the same motions they got away with on other jobs. To be a success in sales you must be "*on.*" It is normal not to be *on* occasionally. As a suggestion, one way to motivate yourself is to look beyond personal goals and see yourself as the newest and most important warrior the Black community has and desperately needs. As you motivate yourself to succeed in sales you motivate the Black community because what you are doing can be duplicated by others. Therefore, you are building a new dream for the community. What the Black community needs is not the love of the majority population but the respect of everybody. Others have shown that success in business along with knowledge and money consistently wins respect. Finally, as we look over our history in terms of our abilities, tools and resources and how they were used successfully in other struggles, it appears that those same tools and resources can be used in our present predicament. The only questions revolve around our beliefs and our "guts."

Summary

The following chapter is intended to give a basic explanation of the sales process. It is the key aspect of this book. However, this chapter was designed to cover some fundamental things to consider before plunging ahead into the sales field. It is not quite enough to be sold on the value of selling. One must understand the changes to and demands upon one's lifestyle and *then* determine if the value of sales is clear to you.

I began this discussion by making the fundamental point that it is very important that a salesperson strongly *identify* with a product and not merely "like it." The definition of sales or selling was said to be so broad as to require more than one set of definitions. I elaborated a bit on the number of ways things are sold and how salespeople get paid. Market identification was touched upon and I explored, to some degree, the kinds of demands that are put upon salespeople as opposed to regular laborers. I ended with a discussion on motivation and suggested that Black Americans are new warriors on the sales frontier - fighting the world of business and the world at large. If all of this has registered, then I believe you are prepared for success in sales.

UNDERSTANDING THE BASIC SELLING PROCESS

The amount of literature available on selling is mind boggling. Virtually all of American culture is based on selling something, so it should be of no surprise that so much has been written on the subject. After seeing all of the books on selling in various bookstores and libraries, one must then realize that thousands upon thousands of corporations have specially developed *their own* sales manuals and training programs tailored for their products and needs.

Fortunately, however, despite the thousands of tons of paper on the subject, most of the authors and trainers agree on many of the basic concepts of selling. This fact makes it quite easy to present the fundamental aspects of selling to you in this chapter. It is expected that as you study and apply these principles, you will develop your own style and approach. Selling is a lot like dancing in that there are basic steps that everyone learns. Yet once these basics are mastered, everyone ends up moving in his/her own unique way. Before revealing the basics of the selling process, I will cover an area that I have called Attitude-Mind set.

Attitude-Mind Set

One of the definitions of selling previously discussed describes it as a transfer of feelings. What you end up communicating will be as much a function of what you believe as the technique(s) used. It might help then, if I may be so bold, to suggest *what you should think*. Specifically, you should understand what frame of mind makes sales happen. Knowing something about how to view the customer is also part of mind-set preparation. With the proper attitude, your communication will be more "natural", thus making it more believable and effective.

a. Feeling Professional

Most professionals usually feel a deep sense of pride when telling people what they do for a living. In one word (doctor, lawyer, engineer), they say to another person, "I'm very bright, I've had extensive education, I'm well-connected, I make a good living and it's all very obvious." The public's perception of a doctor, lawyer or engineer is generally so positive and flattering, that it's no wonder why these professionals can't wait to put their impressive business cards into others' hands. Unfortunately, many salespeople do not think of themselves in such a positive light, and neither does the public. Therefore, many of them are slightly hesitant to say what they do for a living and lack the pride felt by other professionals. This is a mistake. Salespeople are extremely important to satisfying some of the public's most urgent needs, and they should take pride in that fact. Can a brand new salesperson just out of training be expected to feel this way? Perhaps not. But a definite must for the successful salesperson is a genuine pride in his/her profession. What good is it to have a deep belief in the product being sold if one doesn't have a sense of pride as the person making it available to the public.

Another thing you should always keep in mind is that *people want to be sold*. People want to leave a store knowing that they learned a lot more about the item they just bought. They want to know that they were able to compare the various brand names of that item. They want to feel that they properly weighed the benefits of the item at various price ranges and chose the one that best suited their needs and pockets. In short, people want to be assured, through another opinion, that they made a good, if not perfect, decision. And in order to do those things with assuredness, they *need* a salesperson it's hard to do it without one.

People know that the salesperson, generally speaking, knows much more about a product than they do. The only other factor is trust. Can they trust both the competence and the intentions of the salesperson? That is a big part of what you will study; how to be perceived as trustworthy. Once you know that you can make strangers trust you in five minutes, and you successfully show them how to get the best value for the money they're investing with you, you have all the reason in the world to feel proud of your profession and yourself. Of course, making a lot of money doesn't hurt either. In sales, the rich get richer partly because the money makes them feel so confident and professional it motivates them to sell more.

b. Knowing That You Know What You Need To Know

All of us have been in situations where we were learning a new activity and just as we thought we were ready to play or win someone dashed our confidence with a rule or move from out of nowhere. It happens in sports, in card games and in life in general. In sales, your income, your emotional health and a host of other things ride on your successful ability to sell. Yes, it does take time and it is a continuous process, but there are no excuses for not knowing the general parameters of the profession. In other words, a salesperson should be attuned to the specific area he/she is eventually expected to master in order to achieve a level of expertise. Clearly, he/she will have to know how to do more than present a product and handle objections, although they are certainly important. A salesperson who desires success should constantly seek information in at least seven areas. They are as follows:

1. Knowing how to sell - What steps should be taken between the time you meet someone and the time he/she pays you for a product.

2. Knowing the company you represent - What promises can you make to the customer based on the policies of the firm you work for.

3. Knowing the products you sell - What reason does anyone have to buy the product(s) or service(s) that you provide. How will any or all of these products benefit the consumer.

4. Knowing the industry of which your product(s) or service(s) is a part - What new developments are occurring (or will soon occur) in your industry that make this current purchase a wise or poor investment. As a salesperson, new industry developments allow you to

offer a better product or service and to make a greater income.

5. Knowing your competitors - How is this product better or cheaper than a similar product down the street.

6. Knowing your customer/market - To be a good salesperson you have to be able to put yourself in the shoes of the customer. The more capable you are of doing that, the more the customer will be able to relate to and count on you for advice and guidance.

7. Knowing how to finance the product(s) or service(s) - One of the major reasons why people don't buy things is because noone explains how they can afford them. The more ways a salesperson can show customers how to afford, own or obtain the items they want, the more sales the salesperson will make.

One of the reasons why doctors, lawyers and other professionals are admired is because of the great amount of information they have to study and retain. If you study the seven areas outlined above, you to will be challenged to retain a lot of significant information. If you proceed in sales without knowing what you are eventually expected to know, you will greatly hamper, or at least slow down, your trip to the top.

c. Assume The Sale

In sales, it is important to maintain a sense of optimism and enthusiasm so that these feelings can be transmitted to the customer. The best way to maintain these feelings is to assume that each and every customer will buy your product. Why should you assume this posture? There are several reasons:

First, you shouldn't have any reasons to think customers *will not* or cannot buy after you have qualified them. After all, they have approached you regarding the product, or you thought enough of them to approach them about it. In other words, there is a definite *reason* why both of you are at the same place, at the same time, discussing the same product.

Secondly, all of us have been trained, since we were babies, to do what we are expected to do. Thus, if you expect people to buy something, you can be sure that they were programed by their parents, spouses and bosses, long before you arrived on the scene, to strongly consider buying simply because it is one more thing that somebody (you) expects of them. Closely associated with the push to do the expected is the *desire to please*. If a person were to buy your item there is the possibility that two people will be pleased, you and the customer. If he/she does not buy, only one person will be pleased . . . . the customer.

Thirdly, you should assume people will buy so you will make a better, more complete and compelling presentation. If you do not make this assumption, you will make not only a half-hearted presentation, but also, more than likely, accept rather than overcome the customer's objections.

Finally, you should assume the sale because you are a better salesperson than he/she. You see, in most sales discussions that go on for any length of time, both parties end up selling. The salesperson is selling the product while the customer (if he/she is trying to back out of the deal) is selling the salesperson on why the product isn't needed or wanted. The customer is probably not a professional salesperson, however, you are. You should assume that your selling skills will override those of the customer, especially as you learn how to use both logic and emotion to make your points.

You will learn in a very short period of time in sales that it is difficult to separate your true feelings and thoughts from what you outwardly project. Of course, this will vary depending on what and to whom you are selling. In some instances, what you project will not matter as much as in other situations. But new salespeople especially should have some appreciation of the interaction between thoughts and projections. It is easy for a textbook to stress the importance of confidence and optimism, however, I hope that by actually giving you some specific reasons, you might find it easier to be a little more confident and optimistic.

Prospecting - The First Step In The Selling Process

One of the differences between a salesclerk and a salesperson is the responsibility of prospecting. Prospecting is the actual going out into the real world and identifying those persons who would most likely benefit from the product(s) or service(s) you are offering. A salesclerk usually just takes the order of a person who has sought out the store or company for whom the clerk works. Consequently, the he/she does not have to seek out customers. An example would be a department store or fast food salesclerk. Someone selling copy machines or cash registers will probably not experience a flow of people coming into his/her place of employment seeking to purchase or upgrade those products. As a result, salespeople who sell these types of products have to prospect. It is the responsibility of finding customers (prospecting) and *then* selling to them that turns many people away from the occupation. Since most people probably don't know how to prospect, they imagine it to be a lot more difficult than it really is. Therefore, the general purpose of this section is to give you enough information on how to prospect so you will see that it is not as difficult as seems.

One of the benefits of specializing in one area of sales is that you can focus on the particular market that buys your product. If you are interested in selling surfboards, it will make your job infinitely more difficult if you live in Kansas or North Dakota because the people who buy surfboards, generally, do not live in these states.

Successful prospecting assumes that the salesperson knows something about the average customer who buys his/her product nationwide. The typical customer is of a certain age, class, education, income, occupation, residential area, etc. Of course, many customers will not fit the category of those who buy the product (especially many Black customers). But the people who do fit the typical profile have been deemed by the salesperson's company or industry to be the *most likely* types of people to appreciate and purchase the good(s) or service(s) he/she has to sell. Please keep in mind however, that creative salespeople have very often made fortunes by simply ignoring the worn out prospect profile and by cultivating a new type of customer. In this situation, since they were the first in line to sell to this new consumer base, they had the new market to themselves. For example, a few companies were able to get older men and women to purchase what had been known as children's jogging shoes. The older generation had just as many feet and alot more money.

What are some of the keys to good prospecting? Let's start with what I consider to be a very heavy concept. Do you know the single, most important thing that can change your whole life? It is simply changing your intellectual and emotional reaction and response to *the word no.* Usually we stop whatever we are doing whenever we hear that word. There have been plenty of threats and punishments for failure to obey the word no, not only from parents, teachers and employers, but also from the legal, military and political systems. So what happens when we get into the sales field? We hear the word no again and we respond emotionally and send a certain automatic message to our brain because we have been doing it for over twenty years. Success in prospecting, and ultimately in sales will depend heavily upon how you change your response to this little two letter word that has totally limited your opportunities in life. How do you do this? Well, being in the sales field is a very good place to start since you will probably hear more no's than at any other time in your life. Because of this, you will become desensitized to the word. You see, as a doctor gets used to seeing smashed bones and blood and police get used to terrible crimes and murder, you will get used to the word no. The important thing is to stay in sales long enough and to prospect often enough so that you hear the word enough to change your reaction to it. To be more specific, you will have to *change* your response to no, as well as *reverse* your response.Whereas in the past you stopped dead in your tracks upon hearing the word, now you have to learn to advance more forcefully. As they say in the business, "selling *starts* with the word no." With that basic concept as a foundation, let us look at ways and means of prospecting.

a. Cold Calling

This is the most basic way of finding prospects. It simply refers to a salesperson telephoning or visiting someone whom he/she doesn't know for the purpose of investigating or generating interest in the product(s) or service(s) offered. For example, a new real estate salesperson may be asked to telephone 50 people in a neighborhood to find out if they would be interested in selling their homes. Chances are that all 50 people may not be at home, may hang up the phone without responding or may actually say no not interested. Cold calls are often done when there is no valid way to separate the good candidates from the bad within a particular group. So you call everybody, hoping to find that single person who will start the ball rolling. There are long-time professional salespeople who, to this day, do not like cold calling. Fortunately, there are many other ways to line up prospects. Within the last few years, many salespeople have used telephone machines for their cold calls. I'm sure you have talked to a cassette tape in the last year or so, so I don't have to explain how they work. Are they impersonal? Yes. Are they effective? Well many claim that if they get one good lead out of a couple of hundred calls it's worth it since they were productively using their time on other tasks. Obviously, the higher one's commission on the items being sold, the easier one can justify the expense of a telephone calling machine.

b. Mailing Lists

One of the most fascinating aspects of the world of business is its sophisticated storage of data and statistics. Mailing list brokers are in a position to boost your success rate in cold calling because they have people categorized by interest groups. One can match the product he/she is selling with a list of persons or businesses interested in that product. Perhaps the actual nature of the cold call wouldn't change very much, but your enthusiasm and success rate should improve just by knowing that you are talking to someone who is much more likely to become a customer.

Mailing lists are most often used for written correspondence. Many companies, however, also supply telephone numbers for direct dial efforts. A new salesperson should experiment with both forms of prospecting techniques not only to learn both, but also to see which method is more suitable for his/her market, personality and product.

c. Personal Visits

In addition to cold calls over the telephone there are "in-person" cold calls which were a part of the early system of selling. In person visits (often referred to as "beating the pavement"), are when a salesperson drops in, usually without an appointment, on a person or business whom he/she believes has an interest in his/her product. In-person calls are a double-edged sword. If you are refused a chance to be heard you have wasted a lot of time, effort and probably some sort of money. If, on the other hand, you do manage to talk to a decision maker, you have the opportunity to make an impact far greater than any telephone conver-sation or color brochure. Most major companies will not advise their sales reps to make in-person, cold calls. However, if you are in business for yourself, and you must use your time to start the ball rolling, in-person calls may be the way to go. It might be a particularly good idea to make in-person calls when you've sent out printed material and made phone calls, but you've not gotten a response. You may have very little to lose particularly since many managers admire a persistent salesperson.

d. Identifying Past Buyers

If you work for any company that keeps records of sales, you are likely to find a good source of new (for you) prospects. You see, selling is a high turn over occupation. People move in and out of sales positions seeking newer or better opportunities for themselves. What they usually do not take with them when they leave are the records and papers they filled out while working for a concern. For all practical purposes, the persons and companies served by a former salesperson are fair game for whoever has the ambition to claim them. When contacting previously served accounts within your orga-nization, you should introduce yourself, find out the status of their current product(s) or service(s) and try to make an appointment to present them with your company's latest improvements. Hopefully, these old accounts were pleased with the previous service and product quality of your company. If so, you have some of the best prospects one can have - satisfied customers.

e.   Networking

One of the most used words (I won't say overused) of the last half a dozen years is "networking." Networking takes all forms and modes, but the common denominator is the opportunity for business-people to exchange business cards. Usually held in the evenings or right after work at a local bar or hotel, networking groups try to combine a little business with pleasure. While folks are drinking alcohol and eating cheese doodles with one hand, they're exchanging names, phone numbers and cards with the other. Often the noise level, as a result of the many separate conversations, is deafening. Professional networkers don't stay in one spot to long and they resemble presidential candidates in their demeanor, smile and firm, look-you-in-the-eye handshakes. Does networking work? Not usually on the night of the meeting. Networking works in direct proportion to the number of people you have made it your business to meet and, more important, the number of follow-up calls you make. For a new salesperson, network gatherings are usually good opportunities to find, in one place, people of a certain status who are generally in a receptive mood. Small talk that leads to large impressions may be carried on in a networking environment that might not ever take place in an in office visit. Also, because networking is so popular, the traveling salesperson should be especially aware of it. A weekend networking session in an unfamiliar city five hundred miles from home can possibly lead to, say, fifty business contacts in that town. How on earth could this have been possible fifteen years ago?

f. Community Participation

I noted a long while ago that lawyers, whom I'd imagined as being super busy, always seem to have time to serve on a host of boards and committees. "How do they find the time", I wondered. In later years, I realized that in order for lawyers to stay busy they must have a lot of cases and to have a lot of cases they need a lot of clients. To have a lot of clients they must be well-known and respected, hence, one of the reasons for broad community involvement. Not so long ago, attorneys could not do any form of advertising or obvious promotion. It was considered unprofessional and perhaps even questionable from an ethical perspective. For years and years lawyers have used a system of personal promotion that new salespeople can use as well. Every community is filled with churches, charities, school systems, youth groups, athletic teams, social clubs and political causes. Each of these groups provides many opportunities to contribute to the community and to develop a reputation for so doing. Salespeople looking to build an image, serve their communities *and* develop prospects should volunteer their efforts to community projects.

g. Referrals

Eventually you will have some customers with whom you will form close relationships. They will be a key to your growth. If you satisfy them in all the ways that they seek, they will more than likely recommend you to their friends, relatives and contacts. Even if they are not inclined to do so, it is up to you to "pump them" for such referrals. Most people know a couple of hundred other people at least, and you should see your customers as links to these other "potential clients." Sometimes you may have to "grease their palms" with a few dollars to help them remember the name of a cousin who said he was looking for a similar item. But finder's fees are a common practice in business circles and one more sale today could lead to two more sales tomorrow. Paid referrals are usually an acceptable business practice but check your company's policies before you decide to use this tactic.

h. Personal Promotion

Today more than ever the media dictates the tastes of the masses. Television, radio, newspapers and magazines are widely known to virtually all consumers and they get their messages about what to buy from these sources. Though individuals and businesses (large and small) pay a handsome price to get their messages to the consumer through these sources, not all advertising costs money. The media is always ready, willing and able to run a story on an attention-getting person, place or thing. This free advertising is called promotion or publicity. Under given circumstances, usually where the salesperson is also the owner or a major partner, salespeople can generate a lot of leads and prospects by being the focus of media attention themselves. In order to do this, there must be "a hook", i.e., something that grabs the attention of the public, either through comedy, tragedy, curiosity, inspiration or uplifting encouragement. If you sell coat hangers or bath towels this might be rather hard to do. However, many items, especially if they are newly produced in the Black community, may be considered interesting deviations from the norm by the media. For maximum media exposure, a salesperson may have to take on a for-television-personality in order to make the whole concept work. Having experienced a bit of television coverage myself, I can tell you that it works wonders, particularly in the Black community. People who see someone on television assume that the powers-that-be of the all powerful media have checked that person out and have determined that he/she is legitimate and genuine. Thus, the trust level rises greatly through media exposure and many *potential* customers become *actual* customers. Is this an easy thing to do? Well yes and no. Major television networks scrutinize every minute of air-time, so one must have something really unique to offer to land a segment on a major program. On the other hand, many communities have local access cable programs. Although these local shows have much smaller audiences, the new or experienced salesperson can still take advantage of the magic of T.V. knowing that the market being reached may very well be the market for his/her product.

Quantity Equals Quality

I started out this section by stating how important it is to reach a new understanding of the word no. As you try many, if not all, of the ideas presented here to develop new prospects, you will, in all likelihood, hear the word no much more often than the word yes. But selling is a numbers game. One repeats techniques over and over again with dedication and faith, knowing that sheer repetition will yield a crop of potential customers. Quantity prospecting efforts will eventually net quality prospects who will eventually become customers.

The Final Goal of Prospecting

When people indicate a reluctance to become involved in selling, insecurity usually comes up. In the mind of the non-salesperson, selling is a constant hustle where last week's sales and profits have nothing to do with this week's bills and needs. Prior to the professionalization of sales, this idea might have been much closer to the truth than it is today. In sales today, the ultimate goal of prospecting may seem somewhat contradictory. You see, after one has mastered prospecting and has won awards for it, the goal is to not have to prospect again. Why you ask? Because a good salesperson, over time, should be able to make a good living by serving old customers through repeat business, and get new customers from referrals by satisfied clients. A doctor, if he/she is good, will have a practice based on regular patients, referrals by those patients or other doctors. The same holds true for lawyers. They don't have to go out and solicit clients. Similarly, a salesperson who is a good prospector should eventually reach a point where he/she no longer has to actively prospect. The ultimate objective of a salesperson is to get people to purchase that which is good for them. Everything else is specifically designed to get them to that point. The more time a salesperson spends on actually completing a sale, the more successful he/she is. On the other hand, the more time spent going through all the stages (cold calling, personal visits, mailings, etc.) designed to get to the sale, rather than the *actual closing* of the deal itself, the further away that salesperson is from success in sales. Ideally, if a salesperson were to construct a perfect day (and the most profitable one) it would consist of only one activity, closing. There would be no prospecting, no presentations and no objections, just the taking of orders and the collecting of money. In effect, a top notch salesperson might find, in a weird sort of way, that he/she has such a continous flow of customers that his/her desk resembles the counter at a busy McDonalds.

Qualification Of Prospects

Prospects are valuable because they are the people upon whom the salesperson focuses his/her attention. But prospects must be "qualified" so that a lot of time is not wasted on the wrong people. Qualified from a sales standpoint means a person not only needs the product(s) or service(s), but also shows an interest *and* is able to *financially afford* it (them). Many people go into a store or a mall and tell the salesclerk straight out, "I'm just looking." Others will allow a salesperson to go through the whole sales pitch knowing from the start that they do not have the means to purchase the product. They may have enjoyed the presentation, but few salespeople enjoy talking just to hear themselves talk. It's like a fireman's false alarm, harmless in most cases but very irritating when repeated again and again. So salespeople will do themselves, and usually their prospects, some good by qualifying all interested parties. Of course, what is being sold has a lot to do with it. A Chevy dealer might welcome a twenty-year old without reservation. A Mercedes' dealer might approach that same person in a very tactful manner. A Rolls Royce dealer might politely insinuate that the kid is lost and that the Chevy dealer is on the next block.

So qualifying prospects is very much related to the price of the item that you are selling, as well as a number of other factors. Fine you say, how do you do it? Basically you qualify a person by asking them a number of questions in a relaxed, non-threatening way. This is an art that takes some time to learn and some flexibility in order to master it. During the qualification phase you should try to put yourself in the prospect's shoes. You should assume that he/she wants the product, and then focus on the best way of getting it for him/her. If, however, your prospect happens to be a repeat customer or one that you obtained through the searching of old sales records, the qualification phase may be of minimal importance. Unless there have been drastic changes in that person's life since the last purchase (lost job, divorce, bad credit, etc.) he/she is already qualified.

If the prospect is not a previous customer, then you have to identify what similar or competitive product he/she currently owns. This is where your knowledge of your competition is so important. As soon as you find out what he/she owns, several things should go off in your head almost immediately. First, you should register a price of some kind. That is, you should know what this person payed for the product in question (assuming it was purchased new). Secondly, you should know enough about the customer's present product (good, bad or outdated features) to be able to compare it to yours. After you have done these two things mentally, you can then ask a series of questions such as the following:

a. Yes, I am familiar with that model. Which of its features would you like in your new model?

b. Are you looking to stay in the same price range or would you like to move up to something a little better, nicer, bigger, classier, etc.?

If the prospect does not own a product similar to what he/she wants to purchase, that means you have to educate him/her about several things at once, including: operational features and benefits, and total and monthly payment costs (if purchased through an installment plan).

If the product is a major item that will be used by the whole family, such as a house, home furniture, a boat, a car or major appliances, you want to be sure that the person or persons you are talking to have the authority to make the *product* decision and the *financial* decision. Please understand that these are two different decisions. A man may defer to his wife's opinion on any item in the house so long as it doesn't go over "X" number of dollars. If only *one* of the decision-making parties is available, you will have to determine whether you want to go through the product demonstration more than once for the same sale. It is unlikely that you will win many points if you communicate openly or through your actions, "Hey why don't you bring the husband or wife back *then* I'll show you how the thing works." Sometimes you may decide to do just that if you have other live wires waiting for your attention. But then don't be surprised if you don't see your prospects again either.

Most sales books don't ever mention the importance of the salesperson knowing something about financing alternatives. But let's face it, don't most things seem to always come down to money? It seems to for most Black folks I know. If this is the case, then qualifying a prospect really means, given the least attractive financial conditions, finding a way of putting them in a position to get what they want. I am talking major purchases here. Through the magic of credit cards, most people can obtain what they want with two words - charge it! Credit cards have allowed large numbers of people to obtain products that their personal saving habits and discipline would never allow them to own. But what about a paint job for the entire house, a new car, a bank loan for a twenty-thousand-dollar-a-year college bill or other major items? How does a salesperson qualify a desiring prospect who has no credit cards, but who wants to purchase a major item? There are several approaches:

a. Sell the prospect on the most affordable item. All of us would like the better things in life, but our tastes often exceed our pocketbooks. The best victory for everyone is often a compromise. The prospect doesn't get exactly what he/she wants and you, as the salesperson, don't get as big a commission as you perhaps had planned. But everyone walks away with more than they had.

b. Probe the prospect to see if he/she would agree to and identify a co-signer. Because large products are almost always paid for in monthly installments, a person's credit and debt structure are often the stumbling blocks to major purchases. If a willing co-signer who is acceptable to the financing agency can be identified, then perhaps the prospect can obtain whatever he/she is seeking.

c. Consider other creative financing techniques acceptable to both the buyer(s) and the seller/salesperson.

Qualifying a prospect is much easier for those companies that target their products to a specific sector of the general market. Qualifying people usually is a task when products are expensive, and they are presented to the general market. Automobiles and single-family homes are often lost to unqualified prospects.

A good salesperson is not just one who can sell to someone who has an obvious need, interest and financial capacity. That doesn't take any real skill. That would be like giving a person credit for being a good teacher when all the students have IQ's of one hundred and thirty or more. No, a good salesperson, in my opinion, is one who enables prospects to at least have use of a product even when they don't qualify according to the letter of the law. This might mean renting or leasing the product, or selling a used model. Understand of course, that this will have an impact on the salesperson's income. A good salesperson who works with marginally-qualified prospects and does an excellent job at getting them the products they desire, may make less money than an inferior salesperson working with a more affluent clientele. This is often the difference between Black and White salespeople. Blacks have a history of proving they were "qualified" - whether it was to vote, buy a home, or drink from the same water fountain as others. The more "qualified" Black salespeople we have, the better the chances of qualifying prospects disqualified by others. This may not be the key to fame and fortune, but the entire Black community (and the White business community for that matter) stands to gain from our involvement in this aspect of selling.

Making Presentations

Every presentation starts with the presentation of yourself as a person. You must be confident that you "look good" to your prospect. Just about everything in this society seems to emphasize the importance of one's appearance, and your prospect is certainly a member of this society. How one "looks good" is not the same for everybody. In certain situations, the owner of a hardware store, might look rather silly in an expensive suit and tie, whereas a computer salesperson would look pretty strange without one. Looking good applies not only to clothing, but also to personal grooming (hair styles, facial hair, nails, polished shoes, etc.).

It is assumed that most people know what looking good is and that is not necessarily true. In the Black community, for example, some of us may confuse the latest style of clothing with looking good when in actuality an older, more conservative look is more appropriate. In many instances, an individual has to have two different wardrobes, one for personal dress and another for business dress. And, it should almost go without saying that smelling good is as important to your overall personal appearance as what you wear. Body and breath odors can easily turn people off and make them retreat regardless of their interest in your product. Because it is difficult to be an "un-scented" person as some deodorants suggest, it will be to everyone's benefit if you use a lightly scented body and breath deodorant. Your prospect will appreciate that and will have one less reason to be distracted from your presentation.

Before you begin your presentation you should realize that sometimes people do not respond to presentations. Therefore, you should be looking for any signal that your prospect is "tuning out" and adjust your presentation accordingly. Some of the reasons for unresponsiveness may be:

a) They're too busy to listen to your whole spiel. They want you to get to the point. If you don't they'll walk away before you're finished;

b) People are media-saturated to the point that a regular talking human voice is boring, dull, and easy to forget.

c) Customers are more selective or "picky" when choosing their products. The "name brand" item is the one that carries the most status. If you are out of stock or you're trying to sell a lesser known, competitive product, you may meet with some resistance.

d) Prospects who shop several places before they buy a product may have already heard a presentation very much like yours from other salespeople. Therefore, yours may sound repetitive and boring. You have to be creative in your presentations. Perhaps you can use a demonstration, particularly one that your competitors aren't using and that makes the points you want to make.

e) People are more obsessed with themselves today, according to some folks. Your presentation may be geared toward what the *average* buyer finds good or interesting about your product. Some customers aren't interested in those reasons. They may not be interested in why *you* feel it's a good product. They are going to buy the product for *their own reason(s)* only. They may want you to answer their questions first, without, or a least before, going through your standard presentation. You must be sensitive to their wants rather than being overly obsessed by your own demonstration skills.

Once you are confident about your "total" appearance, and you are aware of and sensitive to the reasons why your presentation may be rejected even before you really get into it, you can focus on your "presentation goals."

Presentiation Goals

A presentation has a purpose. The best way to achieve that purpose is to identify it. I have listed some presentation goals with the assumption that some or most of them will be a part of the presentations that you develop.

GOAL #1 To ask questions in such a way that the prospect clearly defines his/her needs or desires so that you can address them. One of the popular images of a salesperson is that of a non-stop talker who never gives the customer a chance to say no, or anything else for that matter. There are, of course, many thousands of salespeople like that, but few would hardly be considered professional. A professional knows that the best chance of getting a sale is to allow people to purchase what they want or need. In order to do that you have to allow them to tell you. Information gathering is a part of almost every profession, from dentistry, psychology and medicine to auto repair. Those who sell a product or render a service want to know what's on the customer's mind and the only way to find out is by asking questions. There is a right way and a wrong way to ask questions. The wrong way is to come on like a prosecuting attorney. The right way is to ask your prospect if he/she would answer some questions. (Just because it is obvious to you that you have to ask, you can't assume that it is also obvious to the customer). After you get your prospect's permission, you should smile to put him/her at ease; almost make it a game so that your prospect won't feel vulnerable after telling you "all of his/her business."

GOAL #2 To really listen to your prospect's answers as well as to note his/her body language (more on this in the next chapter). Salespeople must *prove* to each and every customer that they care about them and understand their needs. Perhaps the single, most effective way of demonstrating this interest is through the quality of your listening. Since customers are not always aware of all the product choices they have when considering the purchase of a particular item, you must carefully listen to them to determine whether another product, other than the one they think they need, is better suited for them. Ultimately, you want them to make the right decision. Your substitute product may be refused. If it is, you should be sure that your customers are fully aware why you are recommending that product. If they are not clear, you should give them more information so they can make the right decision based on those additional reasons. If they are clear and they still refuse it, then you can sell them exactly what they originally requested knowing that you have done your professional duty of suggesting a cheaper and/or better product.

GOAL#3 To include both logic and emotion in your presentation knowing that this combination will get the prospect to act faster than if used separately. Emotion, however, is usually the strongest factor for buying, so you should begin your presentation with logic and end on an emotional note. In order to stir people's emotions, you have to refer to concepts that have consistently aroused strong feelings and concerns over an extended period of time. Some of these concepts are prestige, status, image, greed, pride-of-ownership, color, fashion, style, security, appeal to the opposite sex and health. In order to stir up emotions you must use the right loaded words to trigger the dreams, visions and imagination of the buyer. Logic is addressed in a presentation by noting efficiency, convenience and productivity. Where appropriate you want your customer to see the purchase as an *investment*; one in which he/she comes out ahead financially by acting and purchasing *now* rather than later, when the product will be more costly.

GOAL #4 To try to get the prospect to appreciate your product through as many senses as you can involve in the presentation. In addition to seeing and hearing things, you should make an effort to get the prospect to touch the product, even smell the "newness" of it where appropriate. The more senses involved, the more emotions are aroused and the better the chances for a sale.

GOAL #5 To answer the most common objections raised about your product or service during the course of the presentation so as to minimize or eliminate their occurrence after the presentation.

GOAL #6 To know when you have sufficiently prepared the client for purchase. You must immediately wrap up your presentation and make an effort to close the sale. This goal is crucial and must be done even if you skip some of the others.

Your Voice And Words - Tools Of Your Profession

The readers of this volume are at various stages of development in terms of their readiness to sell. It is rather difficult for the novice to appreciate how much is conveyed about him/herself to an astute or even casual observer *before* his/her mouth opens . Many sales experts confuse new salespeople by giving contradictory information about the value of words. On one hand, there is a lot of literature which says that only about seven percent of communication is conveyed through the words used in a conversation. On the other hand, there is literature which says that words are very important - they paint pictures, arouse emotions, etc. The average person would question how important anything could be if it only has a seven percent impact. What is the key to resolving these contradictory beliefs? The key is the *voice* of a salesperson. The voice can be so appealing that a person hears and desires to hear all the words coming in his/her direction, or it can be such a turn off that a person only hears sound and could care less about what is being said. A salesperson must learn to control the voice the same way a musician controls an instrument. Whether a customer fully understands the selling message depends on how well one uses his/her voice to deliver it , so it is crucial to respect and understand the importance of developing one's vocal instrument. For the novice, this concept might seem hard to appreciate, however, I hope to change that right away by explaining the concept of voice inflection. Voice inflection is the technique of lowering and accenting the voice on words to change their literal meaning. People have to interpret another person's voice inflections. For example, the following sentence has been written several times. If it is spoken with emphasis placed on the capitalized word, this one sentence could have several distinct meanings.

> She did not pay for the dress.
>
> SHE did not pay for the dress.
>
> She DID NOT pay for the dress.
>
> She did not PAY for the dress.
>
> She did not pay for the DRESS.

This is an example of the use of voice inflection and I hope you get the point. Even without knowing the context, you can get at least five different meanings from that sentence. In everyday conversations you use voice inflection to get your points across. As a salesperson you have to appreciate the power of the voice in a new way. In the Black community especially, we have seen how the voice power and rhetoric of our leaders have affected the course of history. From Frederick Douglass, Booker T. Washington, W.E.B. Dubois, and Marcus Garvey, to Elijah Muhammed, Malcom X and Martin Luther King, Jr., we remember what they said, how they said it and how it affected us. As a Black salesperson, you need to learn to use your voice to improve our community's economic situation (and I don't mean by crying and begging).

Your Words

As a salesperson you should want to be creative, and not be a carbon copy of everyone else in your company. Of course, as a Black person you are not likely to be a carbon copy anyway. But because so many people believe that salespeople, like cops and soldiers, are all alike, it is in your best interest to make a special effort to stand out, in a positive way, from the crowd. One way you can do this is to not sound like everyone else. That is one of the few variables in your control. You must look like the other members of your group (dress code), you have the same intent (sell the products) and you use very similar methods (presentations) to get the job done. Somewhere in all of this sameness there should be room for some uniqueness, as long as it brings results. One suggestion only is offered here. Make a list of all the buzz words and sales lingo common to your profession. Words such as sale, deal, price, charge, contract, payment, financing, cost, etc. Write these words on a piece of paper. Then consult the dictionary or a thesaurus and try to find a more pleasant word that *you feel comfortable with* to use as a substitute. For example, when you buy something do you see it as just a purchase or as an investment? Many people don't think they make enough money to get involved with investments. So, if you convince them that they are making an investment, they may feel better about the whole transaction. Words are important because they can affect people in different ways. They can relax or frighten, enrage or humor. Doctors, teachers, coaches and the like all try to sooth and coax people who are going through a trying time. Customers who are about to invest large sums of money may not necessarily be excited about the idea, but as a salesperson you can guide them through what may be an ordeal just by *saying the right words*. If you are using the same language as a less professional salesperson, are you doing your job?

Your Voice

Because it has been documented over and over again that people buy from someone they trust, like, can identify with, or who they feel identifies with them, salespeople must spend a lot of time "buttering up" people. In sales, it is not enough to merely show that you can go through all the correct motions, define all the right terms and fill out all the correct forms. Your success as a salesperson will depend on your doing all of that *plus* pleasing people. I discuss the voice here because it is a key to pleasing and reassuring people. All of us have had the experience I think, of being physically attracted to someone until he/she spoke for the first time. If we didn't like what was being said, we backed off and *ran* away. On the other hand, there may have been a time when you talked with a member of the opposite sex over the phone and just by the tone and quality of the voice (not necessarily what was said) you were very anxious to meet that person. You should realize by now that your voice is vital to your success in sales. People will probably never know most of your good qualities. They will only know you by what you say and how you say it *as interpreted by them.*

I want to state up front that if you are serious about developing your sales ability and developing the ability to control your voice, there will be many other things you'll need to do besides read this book. You will need a good tape recorder, some good scripts to read, plenty of practice and the guidance and opinions of other people. Only by working on your speaking skills, not just reading about them, will you truly improve your talents. What I can do here is discuss the types of things you can work on.

There are six areas that you can focus on to improve your speech generally, and its use in sales, specifically. They are rate, loudness, pitch, quality, voice inflection and articulation.

Rate: I previously mentioned the image of motor mouth salespeople, hopefully you are not one of them. Speaking should be like walking; you should be able to vary your pace from a slow walk (such as you would do in a wedding procession) to a run (what you would do to catch a plane you're about to miss). Speaking, in other words, should be functional. You do not get extra credit for getting in extra words. When you speak too rapidly or too slowly you may be indirectly telling people that you do not care if they understand what you are saying. If that is the case, then they will probably be turned off and therefore not patronize you. To pace yourself in speech you should practice using materials that range in difficulty and vary in emotional content as well as trying different physical environments. Your speech will be slower when you use sales aids than when you are making a straight presentation. You also want to learn to pause in your presentations because it helps you stress points, allows the listener to catch up to you and prepares them to focus on your next point. When people's attention seems to be shifting, increasing the rate of your speech can force them to refocus on you in order to fully grasp the increased flow of words.

You must always compare your own interpretation of how you sound with those of others since *you* are probably not a good judge of how you really sound to them.

Of all the aspects of speech improvement, the rate of speech is one of the easiest to control after one becomes conscious of it. It is important to learn because it impacts people's understanding of what you say and your speed can definitely impact the mood of the listener. Slow speech almost always communicates calmness, seriousness or grief. Rapid speech may indicate excitement in forms ranging from joy to fear. Finally, controlling your speech rate keeps your presentation from becoming boring.

Loudness: If you habitually talk loudly or in a very low tone it is very likely that people have told you by this point in your life. If it is a real part of your character, you have probably seen close friends or relatives do imitations of you and your speech pattern. If either of these things has happened to you, then you already know what your problem is and it's just a matter of your *deciding* to work on it. We all have comfort zones in all aspects of our lives and there is a way of speaking that is comfortable to us: In professions other than sales you would probably be allowed to stay in that comfort zone. Salespeople, however, must care more than the average person about how they are perceived, therefore they must leave their comfort zone, at least during working hours, and better adjust their volume for the general marketplace. If you have a rather normal volume level, you merely need to understand that many of the characteristics of word speed also hold true for volume. Loudness in speech usually signifies a degree of excitement, either positive or negative. Lower voice tones, like slower speech, usually calm the listener.

Not every word in a sentence is equally important. One of the reasons for varied volume is to tell the listener which words or ideas are of primary concern. This emphasis is called inflection and is a key aspect of any sales presentation. Why? Because in a typical presentation you will use hundreds maybe thousands of words. A customer who decides to buy for emotional rather than logical reasons, will remember, or respond to only a few of those words. Inflection is the effort on the salesperson's part to identify on purpose and ahead of time, those words which he/she believes will help the customer make the right buying decision. If you were to speak at a continuous volume level without variation, people would believe that you had the "blahs" - you were non-committal. They would think that you were not excited about any aspect of your product or them as a customer. And you wouldn't want that would you?

Pitch: Pitch and tone are pretty much the same thing and people often confuse them with loudness. The voice is an instrument and just as all instruments have a range of notes and sounds, so does the human voice. Sometimes a high note sounds louder than a low note when in fact both notes have the same volume. Most people that I know do not appreciate high-pitched voices and this could be because they perceive it to be a loud voice. The pitch of your voice is very important because it can give away your inner feelings perhaps more than anything else. It can not be assumed that a habitual fast or loud talker is excited about something once you realize that this is the way he/she normally talks. However, we all change our pitch when our emotions are pricked. As a salesperson you are always responsible for maintaining your goal. It is very hard to sell a client that you allow to anger you or that you anger. Therefore, you must control the pitch or tone of your voice when you are irritated or frustrated with a customer. Many people are not adept at reading the body language that reveals anger or frustration, but most people can hear frustration and the sighs and breathing patterns that go along with it.

Quality: Your voice responds like the rest of your body. When you are confident and well rehearsed you can get into a groove where things just flow naturally. But if you're not confident and you're unprepared, the body makes conscious, timid, jerky movements and the results are similar. If you have ever heard anyone speaking under stress, such as in a courtroom, at a funeral or in front of a large crowd, you may have heard a loss of voice quality. Stress in the neck muscles and vocal cords causes the voice to quiver and shake and the tone could be at either a substantially lower or higher level than normal. This results in the loss of voice quality. It may be the result of not only stress, but also colds, overuse (hoarseness), fatigue or simply poor preparation. The basic goal in sales-related work is not necessarily the improvement of voice quality, but the maintenance of the voice's natural quality. Being prepared kills tension, timidity and nervousness which helps to maintain voice quality.

Articulation: Articulation refers to one's ability to carefully use the muscles of the mouth to form words correctly. Articulation has always been a sign of intelligence. When someone says, "she speaks very well", he/she does not mean tone, speed, quality or loudness. It almost always means that the person speaks clearly and skillfully so that each and every word is understood. Black folks, especially those from the South, are almost always praised if they are articulate. Blacks generally, and those from the South specifically, are "supposed to" speak with an accent, a lazy cadence and almost a disdain for the English language. When one upsets the stereotypical image there is often a dramatic response. "Oh, and he is so *articulate*, he would represent the company very well."

The importance of articulation for Blacks can't be emphasized enough because that portion of this country that has the money you want, *expects* you to sound "colored." If, in fact, you come across that way, there is an assumption that your intellectual development and capability are at an unalterably low level. The English language is a tool, it is not sacred. If people will give you their money faster by speaking one way versus another, then pick up that skill and add it to your resource bank. Now if you have to talk like that all the time, that's another matter.

Articulation, like every other concept discussed here, can best be learned by taking a good speech class, so take one. It would be ridiculous for me or anyone else to try to tell you *how to speak* by asking you to read words off of a page. Reading and talking are two entirely different things.

Other Concepts To Note In Presentations

1. Don't monopolize the presentation regardless of how much information you have to give. Use questions to *make* prospects participate, otherwise you'll have no idea where their minds might be.

2. Summarize your thoughts periodically rather than asking the prospect to give equal value to every word you've said. Give some kind of order to your presentation; numerical, problem-solution, historical or some other conceptual framework.

3. Try to add a little humor to the presentation as long as it's not a stale, dry joke. Humor does a lot to reduce tension and spur trust.

4. Every sales book written in the last twenty years says that enthusiasm is the single, most important thing to have in a sales presentation. I have seen so much false enthusiasm and over enthusiasm in my experiences that I have chosen to substitute the word belief for enthusiasm. But I will have to admit that it is almost impossible to express a strong belief and not be enthusiastic. But generally speaking, *showing* enthusiasm comes from the *head*, *having* belief comes from the *heart*. I think prospects can tell the difference.

5. Use a reasonable amount of data and sales aids. In addition to your verbal and voice skills, there are a lot of other things that will continue to impress people. They include: statistics and figures, maps and charts, videos, reports and objective testimony. Use them as they apply to products, persons and circumstances.

6. *Where* you make a presentation has proven to be a factor in some selling instances. It has been suggested that in-home presentations are most effective in the informal setting of the kitchen rather than the formality of the living room. In the retail environment, getting from behind the counter may communicate an eagerness to share that staying behind the counter would not.

7. When making your presentation, make certain that part of it

requires the prospect to imagine or dream of a realizable situation or setting. Use words, props, and other such things to do this. Try to link the purpose of your product or service with this new vision. Even if he/she leaves your store without the product, by inspiring a new vision you have planted a seed which just might grow and mature. It is up to you, the salesperson, to contact the prospect at a later time to re-establish the dream and offer once again the product that can help make it come true.

8. Be honest in discussing the shortcomings of your product. Don't be so positive that you suggest that it is perfect. By admitting flows you gain a prospect's trust. By gaining trust you increase sales.

Summary

The presentation is that part of the selling process where you explain, for the first time, the benefits of your product relative to your client's needs. It is a question and answer process. A presenter has goals which he/she seeks to achieve during the presentation. Salespeople realize that words and voice control are the basic tools at their disposal, so they take care to master the use of these two factors. They realize that of these two components, the voice carries much more weight than words used. There are at least five different aspects of developing good voice control in sales and each needs to be worked on with the assistance of others and the use of a tape recorder. Sales presentations should include some humor, statistics, imagination (on the part of the prospect) and other necessary sales aides. It should also be understood that both logic and emotion together can best lead people to purchase, however, more emphasis should be put on the emotional reasons for purchase at the end of a presentation.

Responding To Objections

In the best of all possible worlds there would be no objections to your sales presentation; it would be rather cut and dry. Every presentation in that perfect world would be followed by your prospect's decision to purchase. But this is hardly the case as any experienced salesperson will readily tell you. In some businesses, *good* results are when ten percent (sometimes less) of your prospects become paying customers. The first indication of a problem with purchasing your product usually comes in the form of an objection which you hear or sense *during* your presentation. This section will explore the general area of responding to these objections.

Defining an Objection

It has often been noted that one has a problem only if one recognizes something as a problem. In other words, it is how one interprets a situation that makes it either good or bad. Clearly, there is a difference of opinion as to just *what* an objection is, and if, in fact, it is a good thing or a not so good thing. Offered at the outset are some reasonable ideas of what an objection is and how one might view it for the purpose of responding to it.

Objections are challenges to the professional salesperson. A salesperson wishing to improve in the profession will often take pride in taking on the difficult sale just as a star basketball player may want to take the last shot to win a ball game. Selling is the greater part of the business game and the trophy of success is "pulling off the deal" that noone else thought could be done because of the many problems, considerations and objections.

Objections are lessons in understanding the most interesting things in the world, people. It is inaccurate to label people narrowly as good or bad, smart or dumb, honest or dishonest. People are complex. In dealing with objections and how to remove them, you are mastering not only salesmanship, but also your understanding of people and that is *power*. Which is more valuable in learning to overcome objections, the power gained in learning how to persuade and influence people or the financial results of a completed sale? Pause and study this question and your answer.

An objection is an almost unavoidable step in the selling process because it is a direct or indirect request for more information, proof, comparison, logic, persuasion, etc. It is a sign of interest. The alternative to objections would be total silence or the ignoring of the salesperson altogether.

Goals

That phase of the selling process called responding to objections has a separate but very related set of goals which salespeople should note.

a) New efforts to transfer feelings: Because the selling process has to do with transferring the salesperson's positive feelings about a product to a prospect, getting an objection means that that task was not thoroughly carried out. Thus, one objective of responding to an objection is to continue the effort of transferring feelings. This is basically an emotion-based activity.

b) Adding new information to raise value: It takes time to appreciate anything. Unfortunately, neither the salesperson nor the prospect has much of it, so the salesperson has to accelerate the time it would normally take to make a customer understand and appreciate the value of the considered purchase. If a salesperson encounters objections, he/she has to provide more information to make the prospect realize the value of the item for sale. This is a logic-based approach to objection solution.

c) Killing the fear of making a major purchase: What people may be objecting to is the new responsibility they are putting on themselves by making your purchase. If, as a salesperson, you are convinced that it is in your prospects' best interest to buy rather than not to buy, then it is up to you to calm them, reassure them and make them feel secure about what they are about to do.

Why People Don't Buy

In a country where everything is for sale and everything is studied, you can surely bet that the reasons why people do not buy have been thoroughly studied. Essentially, researchers say the prospect either lacks trust (in the salesperson, product, store or manufacturer), lacks the money or means to purchase, is in no hurry to purchase or has no need or desire for the product. After years of research these are the basic answers. If you are a good salesperson who has qualified the prospect, a couple of these reasons should not be grounds for your client's refusal to purchase. It should not be a financial problem since that should been checked before the presentation was made. Also the need and/or desire was (were) established during the qualification and presentation phases of the selling process.

It must be made clear that there is a difference between an objection to immediately buy a product and *absolute* refusal to buy. *Many new salespeople equate resistance with refusal* and miss a sale merely because they did not continue to pursue it.

Objections and Responses

Because there are so many different kinds of things for sale in this country and so many reasons for people to purchase things, it stands to reason that there are many objections to buying as well. Here I present a few of the typical objections and the way one might respond to them. It is hoped that these responses will help you develop responses to objections that apply to your specific business.

1. Price Objection:

Despite the care you may have exercised in qualifying your prospect, you may still easily come across the price objection. Actually, the price objection could be one of at least two different kinds. One objection is, Yes, I do have enough money to buy the product but I don't think the product is worth the money. The second objection is, Yes, I do think the product is great and worth every penny, it's a shame I can't afford it right now.

In the first instance, as stated earlier, you have to make the prospect appreciate the value of your product. One approach, if appropriate, is to sell it as an investment. If you can show that the item being sold is continuously going up in price and that it is in his/her best interest to purchase now, the prospect might be persuaded to buy. If you can show how the purchase and use of the product right now will eliminate future problems and expenses, the prospect might be persuaded to buy. If you can show that the item may be used for more than *one* purpose, the prospect might be persuaded to buy. All of these approaches tell the prospect that money can be saved in the long run by purchasing now. Selling an item as an investment doesn't just mean the item will go up in value, but that it is more cost efficient for the prospect to buy now.

In the second instance where a price objection is due to the lack of money, the situation can usually be approached in at least two ways. The salesperson can either show a cheaper or used product (which in many instances is not possible) or make arrangements for a payment schedule. Other less popular approaches include the salesperson taking less of a commission on a sale by lowering its price, or, by the prospect utilizing a lay away plan. If a customer is not credit worthy (not qualified for a bank card or company payment plan), it could very well save both the customer and the salesperson a future headache by not completing the sale.

2. Lack of Trust Objection:

If a customer voluntarily enters your store, chances are there is already an established trust that the store is a reputable place to do business. What can be questioned is the salesperson, the manufacturer and/or the product itself. Because this whole book is about making you a salesperson and, the importance of establishing trust, it wouldn't be appropriate to say anything more than that you must master your selling skills to be more effective in establishing trust. Regarding the distrust of the manufacturer, you must try to get the prospect to tell you why there is a distrust. If it relates to *one* bad experience you must question (in a tactful way of course) the wisdom of letting that experience ruin the chance to use a whole line of wonderful products. You must also determine whether the prospect is confusing a bad feeling about the salesperson, the store or some other factor with the perception of the manufacturer. A lack of trust in the product usually means that you did not present it well. Perhaps the prospect needs hands on experience or a report or statistics from a consumer's group or another reliable third party regarding the product. But make sure you show your product as it compares to others of a similar nature.

3. Lack of Need or Desire:

Of all the qualities that separate an expert salesperson from an ordinary one, the ability to instill a "desire" to buy tops the list. In the old days, a "pitch man" would come to town, set up a tent or stage and through rapid speech and flashy demonstrations he would virtually hypnotize people into buying. Many of today's salespeople have that same flair, but use a more cerebral approach.

It is not difficult to sell food to a hungry customer nor is it difficult to sell an expensive, beautiful automobile to someone who has plenty of money. What is a good challenge for the salesperson (besides selling something to someone with no money) is to create a desire within someone to purchase something that he/she does not think is needed. The first requirement to meet this challenge is time. It takes time to establish a need time to take the prospect down a road not considered before. But most prospects are busy people and many will not allow a salesperson to have much of their precious time. If this is your situation, you may have to design your presentation such that it is not geared towards making an immediate sale but to set up *appointments* for further demonstrations and explanations. A second approach to establishing a need or desire for a product is to link the product or its use to the universal concerns of people: love, security, health, convenience, status, money, personal looks, etc.

If you use questions in your presentation, and you definitely should, you can often link your product's benefits to a need expressed or established during the question and answer portion of your presentation.

Finally, you must also understand that a salesperson has to be a teacher. Because many people don't know what they need and are often reflections of the commercials they've seen, you must teach them what is in their best interest. You must tactfully instruct them as to *why* owning a particular item is best for them. A salesperson must educate in areas that school systems and colleges do not. But in the end, it is still emotion that activates peoples' "buy" button, so to be a good salesperson you must know how to use your product(s) to stir the prospect's feelings. Beyond the company brochures and presentations, it will take your creativity and *experience with the product* to do this effectively.

4. No Hurry to Buy Objection:

Perhaps the words most often heard by a salesperson are, "I'm just looking." Shopping is a universal pastime, and people often engage in it without a specific intention of purchasing anything. Some shoppers are undisciplined and will buy impulsively, while others will tightly hold onto their money and buy only after being convinced of a need or bargain.

From a consumer's point of view, shopping is a joy when it is free of the hassle and pressure from salespeople. He/she wants to see what is new on the market without feeling obligated to purchase something. This should be easy to understand since all salespeople are themselves shoppers and prospects in their off-duty hours. Thus the "no hurry" objection must be seen, in some instances, as a real situation and not an absolute objection. On the other hand, the "I'm just shopping, looking, in no hurry to buy" rap can very well be resistance from a person who has every intention of making a purchase. Only experience in your area of sales will give you some ability to determine which shoppers are active and which are passive.

The first indication of real buying interest is the amount of time the prospect spends looking at your products, as well as the amount and nature of the questions asked of you. Once you are sure that the customer is actively shopping you can do any of the following:

a. Offer to demonstrate the product of most interest.

b. Offer free delivery or on the spot delivery. The person shopping is looking for a "determining factor" in order to reach a decision. If, after preliminary approval, it appears that the necessary formality of paperwork is the only thing keeping the customer from enjoying the product, you can offer quick delivery, *before final approval.* This will convince the prospect of your confidence in and willingness to please him/her. This could be the "determining factor" that helps the prospect make the final decision. Is it risky for the salesperson? Yes, it is, but it's a ploy that may help *win* more of the close ones rather than letting them get away.

c. Offer to slightly reduce the price on room models. People like to leave a place of business feeling that they didn't just get value for their money, but that they got a *deal.* A deal transmits the feeling that somehow you got a little more than what the average customer usually gets. Offering "sample" products to the in-no-hurry customer may be just the sweetener needed to get some action.

Other Objection Responses

Professional salespeople who have sold a service or product over a period of time have heard just about all the objections there are to hear. Thus, it is assumed that they have already formulated specific responses to these objections and respond not mechanically, but enthusiastically. As previously mentioned, some of these objections should be part of your presentation.

For example, this is what you might say in your presentation: Many people think that they can get a product cheaper at other places and while it is true that they can, what they don't realize is by paying the cheaper price they do not get A, B and C. We calculate that even at our higher prices we save our customers X dollars because we include A, B and C in our package.

It is important for salespeople to quickly learn all the possible objections because it helps to lessen their fears and concerns. When they are virtually certain that the prospect can't throw them off with a new objection, their presentations and responses to objections are delivered with more confidence, which makes for a better selling climate.

Sometimes a salesperson can be so good at responding to objections that he/she comes off as being cocky, arrogant or insensitive. In sales it is very easy to win the battle and lose the war. Communicating will be an integral part of your livelihood, therefore it won't be long before you are able to use words, body language, and other communication skills better than the average person. Do not, however, let your new tools of influence go to your head. You can prove that your prospects' objections have no real foundation in such a way as to embarrass them, make them feel stupid or feel as if they are lying; they would more than likely walk away after your "victory" over them. The main goal of a salesperson is to sell, and *real* winning is most often measured by how much you sell.

Trust, an often used word in selling, is a complicated objection to respond to because it is almost always unspoken and/or denied. Prospects will almost never say, "I don't trust you", even though they may look at you as if they don't. Consequently, many salespeople have no real clue that the resistance they are getting is due to a lack of trust. When there is even the slightest hint that distrust exists, the salesperson ought to do four things during the course of a presentation, response, or conversation. He/she should: make strong eye contact, stand a little closer to the prospect, speak more slowly and in a lower tone. People associate all four of these things with believability. If they are done all at once, the prospect may make a new decision as to the kind of person the salesperson is, especially if what is being *said* is believable, too.

Sometimes a person will balk at buying something because it is not what is asked for. In these situations, I find that the attitude of the salesperson is a key indicator of the amount of respect he/she will have for the prospect.

For example, someone goes into a stereo store and says, "I want a top-quality stereo system with four speakers, AM and FM cassette, Dolby control, television input, and with additional features of A, B and C, and I'm willing to spend $700.

The salesperson can *respect* the fact that the prospect knows exactly what he/she wants and will get the model specifically requested if it exists. If the requested model doesn't exist, the salesperson can do one of two things:

a. Lead the prospect to a model that has *most* of the features and hope he/she forgets or ignores those things initially requested. I personally *hate* this kind of approach because it disrespects the intelligence of the potential purchaser. However, some sales professionals advocate this type of approach. They say ignore some objections or be a little hard of hearing.

b. Say to the prospect something along the line of, "Sir, I can tell you have given your utmost attention to what you want in a stereo system and I really respect and admire that. But at this time we do not have exactly what you want. If you'd like, I can show you something very close to it and explain why it may be a better buy for you, all things considered."

This type of response does several things. First, it praises the prospect's knowledge and judgement; secondly, it notifies the prospect that the product specifically sought is not available; thirdly, it indicates that the salesperson can help the prospect make a new decision (by showing a comparable product) which might be more beneficial. The response you would prefer to be directed towards you is probably the one you should direct towards others.

Although salespeople are told to sell with enthusiasm because emotions are transferable, the greater truth is that they can't get excited *for* others. People have to get excited on their own. A person's own thoughts, mental pictures and ideas about possibilities is what really gets them excited. Thus, it is very important that you learn how to set these elements into motion; seemingly, the way to do this is through the skillful use of questions. Do not ask questions that can be answered with a simple yes or no, because that is probably all you will get. You want to ask questions that will get a person to think and imagine. Ask questions such as the following:

What would you say if I told you I could probably arrange for you to leave here today with the fur coat you have on?

Do you realize how many hours of work in a week you can save if you buy this machine?

When do you think you will be ready to step up to the quality of car that really suits your profession and image?

Logical presentations convince people that they *should* buy. Emotions actually *make* them buy, for the most part, and stimulating questions get their emotions worked up. Understand, however, that there are exceptions to everything. When you go to a hardware store, I doubt if emotion will determine which hammer and nails you will buy.

In response to a person complaining about the price on a high ticket item you should ask the following question, "Sir, do you remember exactly to the dollar what you paid for your refrigerator, your car, your best suit, your boat, or your last vacation?" The answer is likely to be no. If you get a no answer you should then tell the prospect that most people can't remember exact prices because it loses its importance very quickly. What they remember most about high ticket items is whether or not it caused them problems or whether it was a pleasure to own. If they hated the object it couldn't be cheap enough and if they loved it, it would be worth every penny. You can say to your reluctant prospect, "Sir or madam, what I'm asking you to do today is to treat this item as you would the high ticket items I just asked you about. Ask yourself if you would like this item one or two years from now as much as you do today. If you think you would, then buy it today." At this point, you should be silent and wait for a reply.

There are some people with objections and/or personalities that you will not be able to overcome, at least the first time. If you are selling a high ticket item, it may be worth your while to get the prospect's name, address and phone number so that you may get back to them in the future. Many sales are won simply by the continued efforts on the part of the salesperson. Whether it's called pressure, insistence, persistence, determination or whatever, repetition leads to success in sales like it does in everything else.

Learning To Close

In sales jargon, *closing* is asking the customer, in a rather direct way, to make the decision to purchase a product. Closing is not just asking for the sale, closing is actually *getting* the customer to agree to purchase. Failure to close a sale means failing to get the customer to buy. It doesn't take much imagination to see that the close *is* the sale. One can give many excellent presentations, answer all objections, recruit many prospects, etc., but if one fails to close, all those efforts will amount to nothing. *If you do not close you do not get paid.*

This section on Closing is designed to explain some of the aspects of completing a sale. In many respects this is the key section of this volume.

Why is Closing Difficult?

In many respects all the aspects of selling seem rather simple when compared to the challenges of other professions. I am not asking people to perform a heart transplant, save someone from the gas chamber, build a bridge over a bay or erect the next Empire State Building. No, I am simply asking people to help other people do what they are going to do anyway, spend their money. If this is true then a valid question might be, why is selling so hard; more specifically, why is *closing* so hard.

I believe that one has to go back to his/her childhood to get a clearer picture of closing. In your childhood, you were probably instructed by your parents and relatives to be nice, polite and courteous. One way you demonstrated your politeness was *not to ask for things.* For instance, at about two years of age, you learned that nickels, dimes and quarters could get you the candy, gum and toys you wanted. You learned the value of money. At that same age you probably began to ask your parents, brothers and sisters (and anyone else around) for these coins. Then your mother or father told you in very strong language to stop asking for money, particularly from "company" or "strangers." Violation of this command usually led to spanking, scolding or serious punishment. Along with the fear of asking people for money, you learned to *feel guilty about asking* for it also. You see, when a person does something successfully, in spite of being told not to do it, feelings of guilt often arise because he/she has betrayed loved ones. These feelings occur whether one is *caught* in the act or not. Thus, most of you can look back on your early development and find that you were specifically trained not to ask people for money. And you can also remember the feelings of guilt when you did so anyway. The more money you asked for, the more guilt you felt. Many of you were also told never to borrow money either. When you got older and did ask to borrow money, there was a certain guilt or shame associated with it. You were taught that the only honorable way to receive money was to accept it when offered (usually on special occasions - birthdays, etc.) or when paid in exchange for specific work done. Finally, you were made to look down upon beggars, thieves, gamblers, prostitutes and hustlers. In other words, *any* means of getting money except through labor was generally not respected.

Now at twenty, thirty or forty years of age you encounter sales. You see that effort, thinking and speaking are involved, but the greatest emphasis in selling is on closing, *asking* for a large amount of money from a stranger. Despite the value of the item customers receive for their money, your memory bank and nervous system respond and react to those hundreds of lessons given by your parents about asking for money, and obtaining it by means other than "honest labor." And if you, as a salesperson, are *not* professional, then selling does seem like begging. If you don't genuinely *believe* in your product then you will feel as if you're hustling . If you don't have a *system* that you follow then you are gambling. If you are asking for a price that you believe is high, then you do share some of the same characteristics as *thieves*. In short, an unprofessional, unscrupulous salesperson can, in fact, feel the same guilt as other dishonest people.

In summary, people have problems with closings because they are uneasy with the idea that their primary obligation as a salesperson contradicts the teachings they grew up with and lived by for years. Part of "learning" to sell is unlearning or revising some of the values that were instilled by your upbringing. Some people can change while others find it very difficult to do. Sales is a profession that will let almost anyone in, but only those who are willing to work and *learn* (or unlearn) will prosper and rise to the top.

In addition to the influences of early instruction, there are other reasons why people are afraid of asking for the sale. Obviously the fear of rejection is a major reason, especially for new salespeople. In an earlier chapter I said that rejection is not just an isolated event, but, for insecure people it may, unfortunately, be a further confirmation of a long history of earlier rejections. Sales rejections can reinforce feelings of inadequacy and further complicate future sales success. Or, they may have personal confidence but lack faith in the product being sold. What they fear about rejection is the possibility that they have indeed made a mistake in selecting the right product to sell. They fear that the rejections of the public is a statement that a product is inferior, over priced or does not meet a real need. Contrary to popular opinion, you can't sell everything to the public. The same company that manufactures Lincolns used to manufacture the Edsel but they don't anymore because the public firmly rejected it.

Another reason why people do not directly ask for a sale is that if they hear the word "no" they're afraid to say anything else. No has such a finality about it. Some improperly trained salespeople think that if they continue to try to sell after hearing it, then they are disrespectful of or insensitive to the prospect and this they do not wish to be. Others feel that if they continue to sell after hearing "no", their prospect will get angry and direct that anger towards them for continuing the "sales pressure." So rather than risk being the object of this anger many salespeople will clam up after the first no. Because they interpret that first "no" as a sign of failure, they fear hearing it. Therefore, they avoid putting themselves in a position to hear it by not openly asking for the sale. They feel as long as they keep talking there's a chance that the customer will volunteer to buy.

Finally, there are people who have it in their heads that if they try to sell after a person says no then they are begging for a sale. And since their pride will not allow them to beg, the salesperson will flood the prospect with information hoping that its sheer volume will make him/her want to buy rather than having to openly ask for the sale. The salesperson will not offer the prospect more information after the first no if he/she honestly feels they are begging for a sale.

When Do You Close?

In a typical sales situation the salesperson should be in control. The word control here means *most persuasive*. At any particular point in a conversation between seller and prospective buyer, the seller should be able to direct the conversation, or the attention of the prospect in the most appropriate direction. Thus, the timing of the closing should be in the control of the salesperson.

I already spoke about presentations and responding to objections. During this period of time the prospect will seldom stop and say "okay, I'll take it", unless it's an item he/she specifically decided to purchase anyway. If the prospect does not voluntarily agree to purchase, the responsibility rests with the salesperson to *read the prospect and the situation* and determine when to ask for the sale. The prospect will ask questions, inspect the product, ask about price, warranties, etc. At some point it will be obvious that the prospect wants to purchase the item. At that time the salesperson asks for the order. It is important not to waste the time of the prospect if it is apparent that he/she has decided to buy. Many sales have been lost because the salesperson continued explaining product features after the prospect was ready to buy. On the other hand, it is also important that the salesperson not ask for or expect an order before the prospect has a good understanding of the value of what is being purchased. This happens often when a new salesperson gets involved in direct sales. For instance, a woman may go over a friend's house and say, "Gladys, I'm selling stockings, you have to buy some from me." Gladys, who may be a very good friend of the salesperson, is expected to mentally prepare to "give up" some money before she has the slightest idea of exactly what is being sold and whether it is any good. Of course, this same salesperson may not say exactly the same thing to a stranger but she will act, think and expect the sale to take place in a similar fashion. The fact is that the selling process is a process. It can be very short or it can be stretched out. Some steps may even be skipped. But the salesperson should always feel very comfortable that the prospect has an appreciation and value for the product being purchased (even if the prospect knows about the product before entering the store or company). The salesperson should also see to it that the prospect's emotions are heightened by the product. This can be determined by the eyes, tone of voice, rapidness of speech, and touchiness of the hands, etc. Usually value plus excitement plus ability to pay almost always translates into a sale.

Exactly How Do You Ask For The Sale

How you ask for a sale has a lot to do with what is being sold. If a woman is buying a silk nightgown, the salesperson might say, "Would you like me to wrap that up for you, Miss Johnson?" A simple yes or no is all that's required. If, however, a couple is buying a room full of furniture you don't want to make it sound like they're buying a pound of hamburger. You might say, "And when would you like this delivered to your home"? As you might have noticed, in these two examples the request for purchase is indirect but unmistakable. You might ask when they want the furniture delivered, rather than ask if they are going to buy the furniture. But customers know that by giving a delivery date they will then be expected to make some form of payment because delivery implies purchase.

The Choice Between Alternative Approaches

Sometimes people will debate over which of two or more items they really want to purchase. This may go on for some time. They may finally get so uptight that nothing is purchased because the decision was so hard that a choice couldn't be made, even though it should have been. As a salesperson you should help them do what they really want to do, make a decision. You can ask a question like, What is your color scheme now? How long do you intend to live there? Anything which breaks the deadlock is a way of closing (finalizing) the sale.

Make The Decision For the Customer

The assumption that people always know what is in their best interest or will always do what is in their best interest is of course not true. As a salesperson you are also considered an expert, an adviser or a consultant and sometimes you may have to actually tell prospects, tactfully of course, what to buy and then explain your reasons. For example, you might say, "Madame, based on what you've told me you should *definitely* get the XL model. You don't need the ZL model, and the PL model isn't large enough for what you want it to do." Then be *quiet* and let your face and body say "you are going to buy it right?." Most people will almost immediately hand you their charge card, check or cash.

The Tie-Down Close

A long established technique used in closing a sale is one where a salesperson uses a *lingering question* to tie the customer down to commit to purchase an item.

Examples:

Does this shirt come in short sleeves? (customer)
Do you want it if it comes in short sleeves? (salesperson)

Do you deliver after six pm? (customer)
Can I write up your order if we do? (salesperson)

Do you have any cheaper? (customer)
Would you be interested in getting one if I found one more affordable? (salesperson) (don't use the word cheap or cheaper as a salesperson)

The basic principle here as you can see is to answer a question with another question. But the question provided as an answer ties the prospect down to commit to purchase if the question is answered affirmatively. One reason there is a better than average chance of an affirmative answer is because prospects may begin to sound ridiculous to themselves if they are asking questions just to be asking.

Customers Close Themselves

A good salesperson knows that people's egos, not their self-interests often control their actions. The best ego satisfier in selling is to make people feel that they made the correct decision to purchase and that the salesperson was really not much of a factor in the transaction. It takes a skillful salesperson to do this. It requires a person who knows the product and people very well.

Example: A person tries on a suit and looks in the mirror but seems to hesitate about purchasing. The salesperson says, "You certainly look great in that suit, I don't know of a better looking suit in the store for you *do you*?" Customer says, "no." Salesperson, "and the price is right. I don't think there is a better value for the dollar based on what we've seen *do you*?" Customer, "No, I don't." You can pick up the suit this afternoon with the alterations finished. I don't know of anyone who is quicker *do you*?" Customer, "No." Salesperson, "I can't think of a single reason why you shouldn't get that suit today *do you*?" Customer, "No, I don't."

In reality the customer may not agree right down the line with the salesperson. But the salesperson is actually asking a series of questions, deferring to the customer's final opinion. If the customer buys the suit, chances are he/she will think that the buying decision was made by him/herself, since the salesperson just asked questions rather than giving a pushy presentation.

The Investment Close

People have always been concerned with prices since man first sold things to each other. But the recent American experience with inflation, stagnation of minimum wages and workers' salaries have caused more concern than ever before. Thus a major objection will always be price. I believe the best way to overcome price objections is to put an investment framework in the customers' mind. If they are concerned with dollars and cents then use dollars and cents to convince them to buy now.

Close #1

If you are selling a luxury item like jewelry, high-fashion clothing, or exotic sports cars, this close might not work for you. But if you are selling items or services connected to the basic necessities of life, there shouldn't be any problem. The tactic here is to use the reason a person gives for *not* buying as the reason *to* buy.

Examples:

1. A person is informed that an engine overhall for his/her car is needed to function properly. The overhall is priced at about four hundred dollars. The owner rejects the price as too expensive. The mechanic-salesperson says, "Too expensive! If you can't pay me four hundred dollars how are you going to afford a new car?" (The salesperson might also add that the cost is a one shot payment, with a new car the customer will pay almost four hundred every month.)

2. A person calls a termite inspector who confirms that there is a serious problem and it will cost three thousand dollars to fix. "Too expensive" is the reply. The termite inspector says,"Too expensive, what happens when your floors sink after the termites get through? Will you be better able to afford *that* repair bill?" This tactic has to be used carefully as it is very easy to come off sounding sarcastic. The idea is similar to the old oil filter commercial where the mechanic says you can pay me a little now or a lot later.

Close #2

There is a concept in science, business and other fields known as the *reduction to the ridiculous*. It is the situation where the cost of an item is broken down into a small daily expense in order to demonstrate, on another scale, how reasonably priced the item really is.

Example:

A balding man is considering a hair transplant operation that costs five thousand dollars. His insurance will not pay for it because it is cosmetic, non-essential surgery. The bald man says it is much to expensive and not worth it.

The doctor may reduce the cost to the ridiculous to illicit a more positive response. "Sir do you realize that that is less than a hundred dollars a week, less than fifteen dollars a day. Sir, surely hair is valuable and worth a penny per hair. What we are charging you sir is *less than* a tenth of a cent per day per hair." Now the client is not thinking about five thousand dollars. He is thinking about paying less than a tenth of a cent per day, per hair for a look that he can enjoy for the rest of his life. He is seeing the hair transplant as an investment, paying up front, and recouping the value in the future. Reduction to the ridiculous can be a very sound means of explaining value to an objecting customer. If you can write out your "reduction" example, it might even be more understandable, believable and therefore, more persuasive.

Close #3

In addition to the "impending calamity" close and the "reduction to the ridiculous" close, the other investment approach is one where you simply show people how buying your product will save them money on an ongoing basis. People buy smaller cars to save on gas, insurance, tune-up costs, etc. In many parts of the country people invest in insulation, smaller, more efficient oil and gas burners and other products to reduce energy waste and heat loss. If your product saves money it is a problem-solving product and should be promoted as a money saver. Ask your clients straight up, "Do you see how this product can save you money? When would you like to start saving the money that this product can save you?"

As the person answers these questions, their own common sense should be pressuring them to purchase the product.

Third-Party Endorsement Close

As a Black salesperson you are probably always going to be suspect by both Black and White clients. This is unfortunate but it will be the reality for some time to come. For that reason it will be good for you to *prove* your credibility to suspecting customers by presenting recommendation, thank you and appreciation letters. When a person is talking to you one on one, it's one person's word against the other. What is needed are tie breakers, people who can offer objectivity and who have nothing to gain by offering their opinion. Letters of recommendation can offer this assistance. For instance, when a person raises a key objection in a situation that otherwise seems conducive to a sale, he/she should be able to pull out appropriate statements by others to address the objections and/or reaffirm promises and claims. Naturally, these letters and documents don't come out of thin air. You need to contact satisfied customers and ask them to send you letters, on their stationary, stating their satisfaction with your product. They should be included as one of your selling aids. (You will also need a separate letter giving you permission to use their letters for advertisement and endorsement purposes). You can then design closing procedures using these letters. You want to give your client the not-so-subtle feeling of being out voted in his/her hesitancy towards purchasing.

The Emotional Play Close

If a person is clearly qualified to financially purchase your product, the emotional approach would appear perfectly ethical. If the prospect is marginally capable of buying your product, then many people would have a problem with this tactic. This close basically presses the emotional nerves of a person to make a purchase.

For example, a person could be looking at an expensive or quality product which he/she has been dreaming about for years. It could be a fancy car, fur coat, jewelry, or even an expensive dining room table or brass bed. The individual could be like many millions who have scrimped, saved and sacrificed for so long that splurging has almost been forgotten. So after you show your top of the line products and you see the eyes dancing and the mouth watering that person merely looks at you and says, "no thank you." At this point you can look squarely in the eye of the prospect and in a low, soft sympathetic tone say, "Tell me Mr./Mrs. Smith, when do you honestly think you will treat yourself to the (product) that you know you want, you know you deserve and you know you can afford?" Wait for a sincere answer. If an excuse is given for not buying you can ask another loaded question such as, "Mr./Mrs. Smith, you want me to honestly believe that if you walk away without purchasing this (blank), that one day next week, next month or next year you will suddenly come in to buy?" Again you wait for an honest answer. What you want to do is to communicate to the customer that you think that if the product is not purchased from you that day it will probably never be purchased from you or anyone else, thus, he/she will miss out on something that was obviously wanted. You want your prospects to pressure themselves to buy because they, too, believe it is either now or never. Some might call this high pressure selling and it may be, but as I said, the pressure is emanating from inside the customers and not from the salesperson. After all, people do want to spend their money. Professional salespeople sometimes help people, who have forgotten how to treat themselves well, relive those good splurging experiences.

Sometimes the purchase of a product is not based on the pride of ownership. Sometimes emotion may be triggered by a desire for either emotional or physical security. Many purchases are triggered by the need for status, or prestige. If the product or service can be directly linked to a status need (a car phone comes to mind), a person may buy. The more you know about your customer, the more comfortable you will feel about which emotional button(s) to push. Always understand that you must tactfully use these approaches because they can backfire and anger a customer who feels manipulated.

What Do You Do After The First No?

When you have attempted to close a sale and the customer says no, you should have a good idea as to why there is resistance. If you don't know what the problem is then ask. Do not guess, otherwise you might come off sounding desperate. In any event do not panic. Some people always say no the first time they are asked to purchase something. Whatever the reason for rejection, you want to give more explanations and/or demonstrations in the area that raises concerns. If it is a lack of trust in you as the salesperson, you should work on the things previously discussed about voice quality, body language and communication skills.

As you prepare a new strategy to attempt to close the sale, you may want to offer something that makes it easier for the person to buy (accept a super small down payment, make free deliveries, throw in product X or Y at half price or no charge, etc.). While you are willing to make purchasing easier or more attractive, you want to clearly make it known that the purchase must be made today.

Better financing terms (lower credit interest rate) often helps when asking a second time for a purchase commitment.

Under certain circumstances it might work to virtually embarrass a person into purchasing. That tactic works something like this:

"Mr. Smith, we at (company name) know full well that our product is not for everyone. We cater to the discriminating buyer who realizes and appreciates and can afford our line of quality products. I must admit that I misread you totally as I thought you fit the mold of our regular clientele. Obviously, I've wasted a lot of your time and for that I sincerely apologize. May I refer you to (an obvious cheap imitator) down the street. We look forward to serving you to the fullest *when you are ready*. Thank you sir." What would *you* do if you were properly dressed down like that?

There is an expression that says a confused mind always says no. You must make sure that your clients are not confused about what you are offering or *about what their requirements and/or obligations are to you the seller*. Many times people don't understand what they are to do and reject not out of dissatisfaction with the product or salesperson, but out of confusion as to what they are expected to do.

It is very important to have the proper mind set when you are trying to close a difficult/challenging sale. You must believe that you are doing this as much *for the customer* as you are for yourself, maybe even more so. The customer has told you of the problem or need. You understand it and you know you can help cure it. In a sense you are like a doctor trying to cure a patient who you aren't sure wants to get well. You proceed because of a professional as well as a financial interest. It is this professional interest that must be communicated to the client. Many prospects seem to be willing to deny themselves because they don't want to see someone gain financially as a result of their taking some action.

Before your customer makes a new decision, after your second or third attempt to close, you want to make sure he/she has a better image of the product and/or you the salesperson. It takes time to learn about anything. Dealing with objections to a close is just a matter of putting in more time, such as in more formal negotiation processes. One must constantly educate the customer while looking for the emotional loophole to penetrate.

If, after all attempts to close fail, ask the client what you did wrong. You will often find out what he/she was looking for. After this happens, you can get the person's card and start all over again in another two weeks or so. This is persistence and it's always worth something in any game and in life.

Service After The Sale

There is big difference between chasing after prospects in the *hopes* of making a sale, and relying on a stream of clients and referrals which is more likely to lead to sales. The difference is often measured by what you do after a sale. Let's be honest, if you're a sales pro you've made most of your sales by taking your prospects on an emotional high. When these same people get home and unpack the boxes what do they usually see? How do they usually feel? They *see* parts that have to be assembled and instructions on how to assemble them. They also see instructions on operating the product, cleaning and maintenance, getting the factory rebate and the limited warranty card. A few warning labels are thrown in for good measure. Your customers may feel overwhelmed and alone. All the glamour, the tricky store lighting, the rest of the bells and whistles that made for the great show at the store are now missing. The new owners are wondering, almost out loud, whether they blew it again and if they will use this thing.

At this point, most salespeople would not be interested in checking up on their recent customers because it would be asking for trouble. It would be like opening a can of worms. But *you* are a salesperson on the way up. So you make sure you do call your not-quite-satisfied, mostly confused customers. It could very well cement your relationship because it is a sign that you are concerned about them as people. At that point you leave the realm of "sales guy" or "sales girl" and you become more of a consultant. If you sell stereo equipment you become their stereo consultant, if you sell appliances, you become their appliance consultant. In all likelihood, you will sometimes walk into situations where you more or less volunteer your time to solve sometimes simple and some- times time-consuming problems. There is no pay involved for this time spent, but if you do it often enough, people will knock on your door the next time they want to buy something. This is the age of the absentee owner, mobile/transferred managers and minimum wage "I-don't-know" clerks. People will treasure someone who is reliable and will follow-up. If you put in the extra time the first two or three years, your name could be gold to your clients and mean gold for you. Service is time intensive and is not designed for people making a temporary commitment to sales.

Even if no problems arise from your customers you will surely want them to remember you. They won't forget the store from which they bought the merchandise and if they use the product surely they won't forget it. Why should you allow them to forget you. Send them cards, notices, service reminders and information you think they might be able to use. If you can identify their birthdays by all means send a card. You want your clients to see you as someone who is interested in them as people as well as customers. Your name should be in their homes at least once a quarter. Occasionally, your picture should be on some of the literature you send so that face recognition is maintained. If you do these things it will be very hard for your customers not to automatically think of you when the purchase of your type of product becomes an issue. Referrals should also come from these same sources for the same reasons.

It should be noted that service after the sale and prospecting have a little in common. You should keep mailing lists for each, although your client list is the most important. When you don't have big bucks to spend on advertising, it's how you promote yourself.

If your customers do encounter a major problem with the products you sold them, you should try to be their advocate and spokesperson, even if you have to take sides against your own service department. Consumers need advocates and they want to feel that they have an "inside contact" who can cut through red tape. You will probably run into your share of hassles, and monetary compensation will not be immediate or apparent. The reward comes when you start to notice that you don't have to chase people down anymore. They start to come to you, and if you're busy they will wait because they've heard so much about how well you treat people. Actually, you will want to "sell" yourself as part of the package that a person gets when buying from you. Hopefully, you will have an ample amount of "glorious-glowing" letters praising you to the sky as a backup to your claims. So many products today are marketed by a dime-a-dozen method that people have learned to appreciate personal service, if it is available and not too expensive.

COMMUNICATION SKILLS
DURING THE SELLING PROCESS

When a potential customer and a salesperson meet for the first time, there is rarely instant love, appreciation or trust. What happens during the moment they first approach each other to about the time of the salesperson's first closing effort is called communication. In a typical sales training program the training emphasis is almost always on what a salesperson should *say*. Programs talk about what trainees should *say* initially, what they should *say* in the middle, and what they should *say* at the end. It's as if communication is simply a matter of *saying things*. But this is not the case, is it? Saying things doesn't mean a hill of beans if no one is listening with the intention of understanding. Yet listening is seldom viewed as a skill that should be developed like other skills during sales training. Thus, it should be of no surprise to know that listening is one of the single, biggest problems that most salespeople have. And as prospects become aware of your poor listening ability, *what will they do*, they will stop listening *to you*. So you have a situation where two or more adults with very good articulation capabilities and excellent hearing capabilities do a miserable job of communicating because it is based more on talking than listening.

This chapter's purpose is to bring together some ideas, not only on listening but on communication in general. Hopefully, you are humble enough to admit to some weak points and astute enough to identify what they are. If this is so, then maybe some of the material here will help you to more effectively communicate with prospective customers, and people in general.

The first point that is important to respect is that not everyone takes in information, learns, or communicates the same way. I say this point needs to be respected because millions of people *know* it, but they continue to relate to people as they desire and, in turn, expect people to relate to them. They don't respect this point, even though they say they know it, because they still act as if everyone understands and learns as they do. That's like cigarette smokers saying that they should stop smoking, yet continuing to do it as if they don't know that they should stop. Once you respect the point that people learn differently, then you can act on that fact and obtain a degree of understanding that may not have been possible through your normal communication habits.

Essentially there are three basic means by which people take in information. The most common way is visually: people see the world and understand it by watching what is going on about them. The second means is through hearing, and the final, basic means is through feeling or touching. People use all of their senses to take in information; but in the course of one's life, one usually learns to depend on one sense more than the others. We know, for example, that blind people have a heightened sense of hearing and smell as a result of the loss of sight. It's not that the average person's hearing equipment is not as good as a blind person's, it's just that because there is such a reliance on the eyes there was never a need to develop one's hearing to its optimal level.

When a customer comes into your showroom, or you have a meeting with the purchasing agent of a corporation, it will help if you know his/her dominant sense. Does he/she take in information *best* by seeing things, hearing things or felling things. Obviously, what you are selling will be a determining factor. A person buying a five thousand dollar piano will definitely use hearing, whereas a person looking for a wide screen TV for the den will use sight more than any other sense. But in certain situations you may be surprised at what people use. I have read that people often buy new cars based on the irresistibility of its smell rather than its more obvious and more appealing features.

The first task, then, of a salesperson who wants to communicate with a customer is to be able to give a good presentation in at least three different ways. Presentation number one would be designed for the person who is visually dominant. This is probably the way your presentation is already structured because most people are visually dominant.

The second presentation should be designed for people who are hearing dominant. You, the salesperson, are more important because most of what they will hear is your voice. So you have to slow down your normal speech pattern perhaps because the listener is savoring your words just as most people savor a good meal. Obviously, if the item you are selling makes any kind of noise that helps to define what it is, then it should definitely be utilized in this presentation.

The third presentation should be one that will allow your prospect to touch, as much as possible, the item for sale. With this client everything has to feel right both physically and emotionally. This person may very well buy or not buy based on their gut feeling. They will tell you straight out that "something told me to buy it; I had a gut level feeling that said go do it." If you do not take the time to develop these three different presentations, then I question whether you are really concerned about communicating with your client, and you are not respecting the fact that people learn in different ways.

Let's change the subject for a second. You are on a top team playing for the state basketball title. Your coach has told you that defense will win the game for you. He asks you which of the opponent's top two scorers you want to guard. One opponent averages twenty points a game and uses a jump shot almost exclusively. The other opponent also averages about twenty, but he scores on jump shots, hook shots, fast break buckets, driving moves to the basket, and he is a very good free-throw shooter. Who are you going to ask to guard? In all likelihood, you will ask to guard the jump shooter because you have more confidence that you can stop him if you just concentrate on not letting him get his jump shot off. The other guy might make you look silly because he can hurt you and your team in so many ways. Now let's get back to selling.

If you have but one standard presentation (a jump shooter), a customer can frustrate your effectiveness by not responding to your visually-based presentation. But if you develop the ability to score your points in at least three different ways, how could the customer leave without understanding your merits and those of your product? One must be flexible in communication. The person with the most options of how to do something is destined to be either a) the best at the task, or b) the one most in control during the task.

Okay, so you agree that the idea expressed here has merit. Your question then, is how can a person tell if someone is visually dominant, hearing dominant, or touch dominant? Good question. I wish I could tell you a sure way of knowing, but I can't. There are, however, a few options. One can make a visual-based presentation with the assumption that it will appeal to the prospect because, in fact, most people are visually dominant. If you see that you are getting nowhere, you can switch modes. Or you can use all three methods in a presentation, watch to see which aspect of the presentation draws the most interest, then continue using that mode. Or you can ask in a rather indirect way. A salesperson can say something like, "Mrs. Prospect, there is so much I'd like to share with you about this vacuum cleaner, I hardly know where to start. Would you like for me to *tell* you about its features, show you how it works, or would you like to try it out?" This way you allow customers to get involved right away in selling the product to themselves and they will do it using the learning mode that is most effective for them. Try this concept out as one method of increasing your communication skills.

Listening

Regardless of what mode you use to explain, demonstrate or involve your prospect with the product you sell, there will be feedback. Part of that feedback will be verbal. If you do not catch the meaning of what the prospect is telling you, then you are wasting not only his/her effort to relate to you, but also your own efforts to get a positive response. So, two people's efforts (and your commission) will be substantially riding on how well you respond to what the prospect says. And how you respond will be based on what you understand and how you interpret what he/she says. The ultimate question is, how well do you listen? If you do not think you listen well enough, you shouldn't feel too guilty because there are very good reasons for it. If you think your listening skills are OK, you are probably fooling yourself, and the likelihood is that you are just as bad as the rest of us.

There are several reasons why we do not listen very well. First of all, we are not taught how to listen in a direct way. In school we are *taught* how to speak, write and read. But we are *asked* to listen and to pay attention. It is assumed that one needs only to be told to listen and everyone will universally do so and do it well. If speaking is not so automatic, and reading and writing are not so automatic, why should listening be? It is especially interesting when you note that there are times in the day when you aren't speaking, writing or reading. But at what point in the day are you not hearing anything? Probably only when you are sleeping. Logically, then, one would think that listening would be a very important skill to be taught. But such has never been the case to my knowledge.

The second reason why we don't listen well is because our brains can absorb three to five times as much information as the normal human voice can naturally transmit. With so much room left to think about other things while "listening" to someone, it is easy to see why the mind wanders and we lose some of the meaning of the messages.

Thirdly, our values get in the way of accurately hearing and accepting the messages that others send us. If their message is counter to our beliefs, we discount it and have difficulty recalling it.

Environmental factors such as noisy office areas, crowded lunch-time restaurants or loud music in bars, parties or special events can easily distort the words and/or meaning of messages. Often these distractions are unavoidable, so it places both speakers and listeners in the position of being more attentive to each other in order to get good communication.

Finally, for the purpose of this discussion, personal problems get in the way of listening. If you have a physical ailment, financial or emotional pressures or a deadline to meet, the value of what someone is trying to say may be deemed unimportant before it can even get out of his/her mouth.

Regardless of the reasons for poor listening habits, it should be obvious that they hurt the sales field particularly. But you must understand that a habit is a habit. If you are a poor listener, it will affect your total effectiveness as a person, period. Let's look at some of the ways poor listening can shape and affect you.

a.   Access to information: Information gathering is the stuff which makes for progress. In science, in politics, and in career building the more you know the better you can decide and act. Much of so-called "inside information" comes from people you would least expect it. Janitors, bell men, security guards, taxi drivers and lowly office workers often get and give valuable tips. If you are known to be a good listener, *people will tell you things*. They will tell you because they will not consider it pointless or wasted effort and it may have some value later on. But if you are known to ignore people or to be a poor listener, then you may be missing out on important tips because people will think "what's the use, he/she doesn't listen anyway, why bother."

b.   Less influence, respect and attention when speaking: In an office environment where people interrelate on a daily basis and everyone learns the personalities of his/her co-workers, it is very bad to be perceived as a poor listener. A poor listener often will not get much attention, respect or credulity when speaking for at least two reasons. First, to listen to someone is a courtesy; one does not have to do it. Thus, if your co-workers universally perceive you as a person who has not been attentive to *their* ideas, problems and conversations, why should they give you the courtesy of listening to you. Secondly, if it is common knowledge that you are a poor listener, then it will also be assumed (rightly or wrongly) that "you really don't know what is happening." Who listens to someone if it is believed that that person doesn't know what the heck is going on anyway? Poor listening will very likely affect how you are perceived and received as a speaker. A good listener draws people because they want to know what he/she's heard.

c.   Forgetful: A poor listener has poor recall. Scientists say that we forget half of what we've heard within eight hours and eventually ninety-five percent later on. People will also confuse, exaggerate or otherwise distort what they do remember. A part of what they remember they do not believe, rendering that information virtually useless anyway. These figures are said to be for average people, poor listeners are said to be worse. If in your work situation you are a poor listener, it can be assumed that there will be many things that you will not recall. You won't be able to recall them because you were barely listening when they were first expressed. In any event, you could develop a reputation for being very forgetful. And in many instances a forgetful person is viewed as irresponsible and untrustworthy among other things. Could a reputation like this hurt your chances for advancement?

d.   Poor sales: Up to this point, I have related poor listening skills to the daily interaction of people working together. In sales you usually get only one good shot. If your prospect feels that you are not listening, he/she is very likely to walk away in disgust. You can't afford to have that happen too many times.

Improving Listening Skills

The following hints are being offered for the express purpose of assisting people in becoming better listeners. While it is good to keep them all in mind, it might be more practical to identify the two or three areas that you feel you are in most need of improvement.

a.   Have a purpose for listening: Most good listeners are naturally curious people. They love to absorb information from all sources and just add it to their general memory bank. If you are not that way, it's all right. But when asked to listen to someone, try to give yourself a specific purpose for listening to that person. Purposeful listening is better listening.

b.   Pay attention to voice inflection: I have already demonstrated how the same sentence using the same words can have several different meanings depending on how the voice is used. To get the true meaning of what's coming at you, take heed of voice inflections. And if there is doubt, ask questions.

c. Do not interrupt, let a person finish what he/she is saying: The most anger-provoking thing that a listener can do to a speaker is to interrupt before he/she finishes, particularly if the practice is habitual. The listener may as well tell the speaker "shut up, you have nothing important to say." Interrupting a speaker is usually a sign of an insecure, provoked, or tired listener, as well as disregard for the speaker. Avoid this habit at all costs, especially in sales. If you are not understanding what a person is saying, wait until he/she stops talking and then ask for a further explanation.

d. Do not plan your rebuttal while a person is still talking: Most people often do not completely hear what another is saying because they are planning their rebuttal while the other party is still making points. The usual excuses for doing this are: a) "I'll forget my point if I don't say it right away", or b) "I knew what was going to be said before his/her mouth opened." But let me ask you a question. What is the most flattering thing you can do when someone has just spoken to you? The answer is usually to be silent for a few moments. When you do this you are saying several things. You are saying (or leading the other person to think), "you have given me something to think about"; "I never considered that"; "That is an interesting point." When you are silent you are telling the speaker that something profound was said, and that is what people like to think that they are able to do. Now if you reply after the silence, the former speaker will listen to you much more intensely because: a) he/she believes you have thoroughly listened and considered his/her point, and b) you may very well say something important or profound yourself since you will be responding to his/her profound statement. The former speaker wants to make sure that what you say is heard. If not, then his/her statement was wasted. Communication is like money. People usually insist on an equal exchange.

e.   Do not "go off" in response to emotionally-charged words: Have you ever noticed that everyone praises the smooth, cool operator. In sports, in war, in business and even in poker, people respect those individuals who minimize the expression of emotion. Why? I guess because most people have concluded that efficiency is the best policy and emotion usually gets in the way of people doing their best. If you get upset during a conversation (before that conversation is completed), you may miss out on other information or facts that may clue you in on how to deal with the upsetting situation. It's really like being a basketball coach. If a coach gets two technical fouls he is out of the game and unable to finish coaching the very game that he was so emotionally involved in. If his team eventually loses, he will have paid twice for his emotional outburst.

f.   Be polite, even if uninterested; ask a question to change the topic: Let's be truthful. There are many times when you just know that there are things more urgent to deal with than listening to what someone wants to tell you. Even in a sales situation a prospect may want to take you out in left field to discuss a sports team or a local controversy. What do you do? You ask a question. In asking a question you are still telling the speaker that you want to listen and that you want him/her to continue talking. All that you are doing is either changing the topic or getting more to the point on the same topic. In effect, a question is a compromise. You have interrupted the speaker's intent, but you have not said that what was being said is unimportant. The more tactful and polite you are in making this move, the less offended the speaker should be.

g.   Put personal problems on the back burner: Everyone has problems and they usually span the course of one's life. How people function in life is related to not only to the number and seriousness of problems, but also to the response to these problems. Engaging people in conversations for the purpose of obtaining a financial commitment is no time to think about one's problems. When people are buying something of any significant cost, they want the salesperson to focus on them. They want every question answered, every assurance made, every guarantee explained, every smile given and every service provided. You, as the salesperson, cannot do that if you are steeped in your own web of problems. If you care about your image, and if your problems are that great, maybe you should not report to work that day and foul up your image. Or maybe you should spend that day doing paperwork, making new plans or less important phone calls. People like dealing with someone who projects a strong image, someone they admire. In our culture, a strong person is not supposed to expose his/her problems for the world to see. Unfortunately, there were certain rules established before you decided to get into this game and this is one of them.

h.   Leave noisy settings: In many films I have seen, there have been scenes of the newsroom of a large newspaper. All I could see was a big open room without dividers or cubicals and a hundred typists and writers hammering away on noisy typewriters. I used to wonder how anyone could work in that kind of environment. But thousands of people do work in crowded, chaotic situations, yet communication still goes on. If your selling situation is noisy (as on the floor of the stock exchange), you will have to do the best you can. But when possible, you should try to remove yourself and your client from unnecessary noise and interruptions in order to: a) improve the chances of properly hearing what the other person is saying, and b) show a general consideration for your client by moving them to a more hospitable setting. How can a person open up if there is every reason to believe that you cannot hear him/her?

i.   Read between the lines: Very often people want to relate an idea without actually spelling it out. They would rather hint at it, hoping that you will pick up the message. Why would someone do that? Maybe because it's embarrassing to actually say what he/she means, but it's a situation where the flow of ideas must not be interrupted. For example, a woman walks into a store that sells fur coats. She walks over to the full length coats and notices the price tags. By the time you come over, she asks you, "Do you have this coat in a jacket length, I really don't think I need a full length coat?" Now there are at least two ways you can read this statement. You can assume that she *does* want the full length coat but it is beyond her budget, so she is asking for a jacket, which she thinks she can afford. Or, she might mean exactly what she said. She likes that particular fur but desires it in a shorter version. She might also try to set you up by looking at a host of other coats, expressing interest, then coming back to the original coat, hoping that you will lower the price to one that she can afford. Learning to read between the lines is especially important in sales, because in most cases the two parties have just met, they want to walk away thinking that they got what they wanted out of the purchase. They are under no obligation to tell all during this relatively short meeting. Thus, reading between the lines is a valuable skill to have. Part of sales success is based on assuming the sale. The better a person can read between the lines, the better ground he/she stands on in making certain assumptions.

j.   Notice what is not said: This concept is very similar to reading between the lines, but it is distinct enough to merit separate categorization. In normal communication you are trying to read the other person's intent as you listen to his/her message. The two functions are related but distinct. As a salesperson you are trying to get prospects to appreciate your product to the extent that they want it. You use words to get to this point. They use words in response to your words, and then they advance some words of their own. Meanwhile, between the exchange of words you are trying to read their intent. Sometimes many prospects' words are in direct conflict with what you read as their intent. In some of these instances you have to somewhat reverse yourself and judge them by what they have *not* said. Sometimes customers play with or test salespeople. They make objections to buying; they articulate the reasons why they shouldn't buy the item, but they never say *"no I won't buy!"* There is no finality to their series of statements. When it seems clear that they will say everything but no, you have to assume the sale and make the close. At that point, the truth will become known.

k. Take a Class: Although I have given several hints on how to improve your listening skills, a class on the art of listening should definitely be considered. Think about all the classes you have taken in your life already. Have they served you as well as a class in listening might? It might be important for no other reason than to test yourself before and after. The hints offered here will depend on your personal self-discipline, which may or may not respond to the improvement challenge. But any decent class on the subject should be able to tell you how good or bad you are right now, and then measure your progress over a period of time. Consult your company, local university or a speech and drama group for local opportunities.

It is important when you embark on your improvement program to note your results. They may not be very apparent to you, but there are ways you can measure your progress. The best means of measurement should be through improved personal relations and improved sales. As I see it, the biggest benefit of better listening to you, the salesperson, is that it makes you a better customer analyst. Because you are hearing and understanding more, you are receiving more information with which to help your prospects make a decision. You will understand their dilemmas better, and hear, as you read between the lines, what they like, dislike and why. And as you listen better, it will be noticeable to your customers because they are looking for someone to listen to them. As they notice that you are listening, they will feel you care, because it is very difficult for them to separate the two. A caring person is easier to trust than an uncaring one; so if there is any possibility that your prospects are qualified to buy, they will likely buy from you.

The final benefit of all of this is that it can become habit-forming. As you see the benefits of better listening, you will likely continue to make the effort to listen. The benefits of listening are not just limited to better personal relationships, more sales and income, although that would be enough. Better listening leads to more creative capability on the part of the listener because he/she is seeing things in a broader perspective. The listener is more objective and less opinionated. And these creative and perspective improvements greatly enhance a salesperson's ability to negotiate and compromise. After all, aren't selling, negotiating and compromise all fruit from the same tree?

Observing NonVerbal Communication

The last aspect of communication that I will cover in this section is that area referred to as non-verbal communication, also known as body language. It is interesting to note how researchers try to break things down into percentages at every opportunity. I have read where only seven percent of the meaning of a statement is captured by the actual words used. Another percentage is conveyed by the inflection and/or tone of the voice, while another percentage is relayed through facial expression. For our purposes it is unimportant to memorize percentages (it would probably vary from person to person anyway), as long as one realizes that the actual words used in a statement are only a small part of the message being transmitted. I have already reviewed how voice inflections and accents noticeably change the meaning of words. Now I will examine non-verbal messages.

Customers come in all varieties, with many motives and drastically different pocketbooks. But it would be pretty fair to say that most customers come into a buying situation with what psychologists call an approach - avoidance syndrome. What that simply means is that they have mixed feelings regarding what they are about to do. One part of them says *go buy* while the other part may say *wait awhile* or *hold on to your money*. Just because they have left their homes to come to your place of business, or allowed you to come to their homes or offices, does in no way mean that they have decided to buy. Thus, when you meet a prospect, which you can usually do only with his/her permission and cooperation, you could very well be talking to a confused person who is sending you mixed and contradictory messages. When confronted by this confusion you have to do at least two things. First, you have to accept the normalness of having mixed feelings; it should not confuse you as to why your prospect is confused. The second thing you have to do is decide which side of the confusion you are going to target in terms of your own presentation. You have to get your prospect out of a confused state, and you have to be able to recognize when you are doing it *as* you are doing it in order to be effective. It is at these points that knowledge of body language is important. Your ability to observe your prospect's reactions to your actions should alert you as to whether to proceed along the same path or change your approach, language or learning mode.

Observing The Prospect's Body Language

Nonverbal communication or body language is not a totally foreign concept to any of us. We each use it and note it in varying degrees, forms and levels of accuracy. Perhaps you became aware of your own body language when, as a youngster, your parents told you, "You'd better stop rolling those eyes or sticking that lip out or I'm going to smack your face." Perhaps it was at that point in your life that you realized, without saying a thing, you could still get into a lot of trouble merely by showing with some small part of the body how you felt about a statement or an order.

Today most of us pay the closest attention to body language when talking to a member of the opposite sex. Conversations between men and women reveal over and over that the word *no* might really mean yes or maybe, depending on how it is said and the accompanying body language. As a salesperson it will be crucial for you to develop a higher degree of both sending and interpreting various forms of body language. A fundamental use of language and communication is as a negotiation tool, and certainly negotiation is a standard aspect of buyer and seller communication. For example, in negotiation, the buyer may use a nonverbal tactic to get the seller ("opposition") to propose what the buyer desires. If the buyer (through the use of gestures, for instance) can get the opposition to make such a proposal, then he/she is most certain to get it and do so without argument, haggling or fear of rejection.

The most widely used body part in nonverbal communication is the face. A "no" with a smile is usually significantly different from a "no" with a blank face or a "no" with a squinting face. The former might mean "maybe," whereas the latter two might mean "I really don't understand what you are saying, so I say no for right now until I understand you", or, "I'm not interested in buying at all."

It is the eyes that reveal the most about most people. An enlargement of the eyes could mean fear, excitement or surprise. Squinting eyes usually mean confusion, fatigue or anger, whereas rolling eyes could mean anger or frustration. A major reason you want to master reading body language is because when there is conflict between what a person actually says and how they really feel, body language is usually a more accurate indicator. Thus, the better you read body language, the better your chances of getting at the truth.

There are several reasons why you can't always trust what people say. The first reason I have already identified: genuine confusion on the part of the buyer as to what is in his/her best interest. The other reason is that we are taught to be little liars and not to reveal our true feelings. People have been told, "Tell them whatever they want to hear." This is sometimes considered more of a courtesy or being supportive than actually lying. "Don't ask stupid questions" is another thing people are taught that prevents them from admitting that they are confused. "Don't show everybody how dumb you are" is another teaching. Finally, there is the deep feeling, which may be justified because of past practices of unethical salespeople, that if you do reveal your true feelings about an item that you are looking to buy, a salesperson will exploit that feeling and overcharge you. Because of fear of exploitation, fear of looking stupid, simple courtesy or genuine confusion, people will often not verbalize their true feelings. If you can't make a distinction between what a person says and how they actually feel, you will miss many opportunities to educate them. Without your important input, your customer will either defer making a buying decision or make an incorrect buying decision. Neither of these outcomes is to the advantage of the salesperson nor the customer.

OK, you say, this all makes sense, but you can already do these things, right? But the difference between reading body language in the ordinary course of events and reading it as a salesperson is *response*. Your livelihood may not depend on how well you read nonverbal communication as much as it does if you are in sales. It is an essential part of selling. You must learn how to interpret the nonverbal movements you are observing, as well as master how to make the right gestures, and nonverbal movements so that your prospects will be influenced by more than just what you say.

In everyday communication, when a person's nonverbal and verbal patterns are inconsistent, you usually ignore or challenge, in a rather direct way, what he/she says. You might let it be known that you don't think he/she meant what was said, and in so doing risk whatever is at stake in the conversation. As a salesperson you cannot do either of the above. You cannot ignore what people are saying just because they are confused, and you certainly can't tell them in so many words, "I think you are lying." You must be professional, yet responsive to what you are observing. You must tactfully supply them with additional information so that they can reconsider or make an amended decision without feeling ignored. You have to scratch them where they itch (exactly where they itch) without them telling you where they itch. A salesclerk will not be expected to do this but a professional salesperson will. A salesclerk usually doesn't influence the decision(s) of a customer, they simply wait for the customer to make up his/her mind, and take the payment.

Another part of nonverbal communication is dress and appearance (although probably less so in California). Although people in blue jeans do seriously shop for Rolls Royces and mansions, generally speaking, a very poorly dressed person may not be a qualified prospect in many retail settings. A salesperson may have to make this kind of a subjective decision when he/she is swamped.

You also have to learn to read the many nonverbal messages that husbands and wives send each other during your presentation. Perhaps the wife thinks the product is too expensive. She wants her husband to get that message without saying it because she doesn't want the salesperson to pounce on her with a long treatise. So she sends her husband a nonverbal gesture that says the price is too high. You, as salesperson, have to be able to read that message, even though it was not sent to you, because it affects you. You have to respond to her belief that the price is to high even though she never said a word. You have to address both of *them* on that issue so the wife will not feel attacked and defensive.

The final aspect of nonverbal communication that salespeople should consider is that of personal space. The farther away you are from someone physically, the less effective the communication because the listener perceives you as being distant. The closer you are to a person, the more influential you usually are. In our culture there certainly are limitations as to how close you should get to a person, and only by constant testing and experimentation will you learn what is the best distance for you.

In summary, a prospect's body language is the real key to his/her thinking, concerns, doubts, etc. A professional salesperson is a "people analyst" and *reads* them for the purpose of helping them make a buying decision that is in their best interest. After a salesperson notes body language, he/she will supply information in a tactful, relaxed way either to build up emotions that will lead to a buy or to reduce emotions that are preventing one. Like almost everything else in America, there are books and classes on this topic, and it may make you a more successful salesperson if you check some of them out.

The Salesperson's Body Language

Body language utilization has an even stronger implications for salespeople than for the public at large because they must be effective persuaders. In sales, you must use body language to fortify your verbal message. Your prospect is "checking you out" as you make your presentation and answer questions. Your body language is being read just as you are reading that of your prospect. He/she may, in fact, be a salesperson, lawyer or police officer and may be more experienced in understanding body language than you are. So in your sales career you want to make sure that your body and mouth are in sync. Essentially, customers are looking for a least three things when reading you, the salesperson. First, they note whether you know what you are talking about. This is basically determined by what comes out of your mouth. After they see that you seem to know what you are talking about, they look to see if you seem honest, truthful and sincere. Finally, they want to see if you are listening, understanding and paying attention to what *they* are saying. These last two things are conveyed to customers more through their *interpretation* of your body language than anything else. I use the word interpretation purposely because some people have natural body moves that mean one thing to them but mean or say something else to others. Thus, if you want to be more effective with the public, you may have to change some of your natural movements so as not to be misread or misinterpreted.

How does a salesperson ensure that his/her body and words work as one. Well, the secret was spelled out much earlier in this volume: *belief.* Because your mind and body are so firmly linked, it is very difficult for the body to do anything that the mind doesn't conceive or believe. Thus, if you believe in your product, your body will tend to flow in the direction of your belief. If, after you have sold the product for awhile, you begin to question or lose faith in the product's capability or the company's sincerity, it will likely be noticeable, to an astute observer, in your voice, and through your nonverbal communication. This is why belief in your product is so important. You will fool some of the people some of the time, but you can't depend on making a living fooling most of the people most of the time.

You should be in control of your body language and your nonverbal skills. You should know how to send a broad range of messages using all parts of your body, and you should know when to do it. You should also know exactly what you look like when you are sending your messages. I hate to use the word actor, because it almost has "unreal" or "unsincere" connotations, but you should be like one who watches him/herself on the screen and *likes* how he/she appears to everybody else. You must like what you see, and it must be effective in closing sales and earning you a desirable income.

In today's modern world of training techniques, you can watch yourself perform thanks to the magic of videotape. Someone should tape you both in training and in real sales situations, and you should study yourself the same way a football team studies tapes of the previous Sunday's game. You should ask yourself some questions. Do I like the way I look and come across? Am I smiling enough? too much? in a relaxed way? strained way? What is my body language saying? Can it be better? How? Is there anything that I do that is unexpected or unnatural? What about my posture, hair, weight and eye contact? Am I nodding in agreement mechanically? too much? not enough? naturally? etc. Can I look older or younger if I need to? I have said before that the expectations and assumptions you carry around in your head will influence your success rate in sales. You may want to ask yourself if you look like you assume the person is going to buy. Are you putting out some degree of obligation to the customer?

There is little question that an in-depth look at oneself in action is extremely instructional. Hopefully, you have a group of peers who are striving for excellence in sales also, and they can help you positively critique your style and say what kinds of messages they see or fail to see. This is an obvious action activity where book smarts is no substitute for performance.

In addition to concepts I have mentioned thus far, what other factors should you consider in your nonverbal communication?

a. Appearance and weight: Overweight people have two images. One view is that they are out of control, undisciplined, sloppy, and slow - all these factors bring on the excess weight and cause it to continue. The other image of fat people is that they are happy-go-lucky folks who can always laugh at a joke, if not make one. The former image is growing while the latter is fading. Outside of being a Japanese wrestler, there are few positive impressions of overweight people. Without mentioning the health benefits of a slimmer body, it is in the best interest of salespeople *not* to be overweight. Remember, it is the customer's opinion and not the "facts" that count in most sales situations. In case you didn't know, salespeople have to cater to the customer, not the other way around.

b.   Age: In selling certain items, a young salesperson may not appear to the customer to be old enough to know a great deal about the product being sold (for instance, houses or cars). If a prospect is not sure about parting with a good deal of money and taking on the responsibility of monthly payments, it is of little comfort to be waited on by a person that is perceived to know even less than he/she does about the product. Thus, a young person may seek to project a very conservative image to add credibility while an older person may want to make his/her wardrobe more up-to-date and stylish. Of course, if you open your mouth and either sound like a baby or an ancient wise man then it almost defeats the image building.

c.   Mirroring: Mirroring someone combines both the verbal and nonverbal aspects of relating. The purpose of mirroring is to get a prospect to relate to you as an equal to maximize the flow of information. Mirroring means, for all practical purposes, doing what your customers do in the way that they do it. If they talk fast, you talk fast, if they have their hands in their pockets you may eventually put yours in your pocket. It is important that you do this naturally and over the course of the conversation. The prospect should feel that "you and he/she are alike and on the same level." This ability to identify should make it easier for the person to proceed with a purchase. If you fumble the ball, and mirror in a poor way, the customer will take notice and assume that you are making fun, and he/she will leave in disgust. Is this selling idea for everybody? No, it isn't, and it isn't to be used in all situations. But for salespeople who are masters of the basic skills and looking to add to their techniques, this concept could very well make a positive, financial difference.

d.   Master your face: In addition to your smile and head nodding, what other expressions can you demonstrate at will? What is your serious look? your surprised look? your I'm impressed look? your sympathetic look? Develop and expand your range of looks and use them in your presentation and responses. If you don't think this makes sense, then you might have doubts about your belief in your product or your interest in and tolerance of people. Or, you might not understand that a *professional* salesperson has to do more than *be natural*. If that weren't the case, then *all* natural acting people would be professional salespeople and wealthy, too. If controlling your facial muscles seems like *going through too many changes, then compare* these changes with those needed to be a doctor or lawyer.

e. Use your hands: It was previously mentioned that some people do not learn well by listening but rather by watching. Thus, it is important that salespeople learn to be very expressive with their hands while demonstrating or showing a product or service.

I have used the word process over and over again in connection with selling. Learning nonverbal communication is an obvious example of why we use the word process. One cannot master reading or using non-verbals in a short period of time. It can only come through extended practice, use and study. It comes from a desire to understand and influence people. Hopefully, the hints offered here will be added to your other selling skills, and you become the professional you have the potential to be.

Other Books Available from VSBE Include:

BLACK FOLKS' GUIDE TO MAKING BIG MONEY IN AMERICA

After 7 years and better than 60,000 copies sold, **BLACK FOLKS' GUIDE TO MAKING BIG MONEY IN AMERICA** continues to find its way to the personal libraries of self reliant Black Americans.

BLACK FOLKS' GUIDE TO MAKING BIG MONEY IN AMERCA was written to answer many of our most pressing financial questions. topics include job searching skills, credit counseling, home buying techniques, bargain shopping, time management, saving plans, income tax strategies and much, much, more. There is a review of the 24 principles that virtually all wealthy Americans use to develop and maintain their wealth. There is a chapter discussing the 13 roadblocks that keep black Folks in continued poverty.

This publication deals with the special financial problems of the single Black female parent. It discusses the relationship of Black Folks to land (real estate) and business.

The most important and innovative aspect of this work is that it includes a STEP-BY-STEP PLAN OF ACTION designed to instruct the serious Afro-American how to increase their wealth and improve their lifestyle.

BLACK FOLKS' GUIDE TO BUSINESS SUCCESS

Black Folks' Guide to Business Success tells the reader what practices to use and which practices to avoid in establishing a stable enterprise. The information is presented in a clear and understandable style that makes for easy and enjoyable reading.

Other topics covered in this book include:
- Specific business ideas for the Black community - What, Why and How Much?
- A discussion of Black People's attitudes towards money. Do they help or hinder the quest for the dollar?
- A discussion of black business attitudes. Do Blacks go into business to make money?
- The true cost of establishing o successful business. Besides money and time, what are other costs?
- The Black Brain Drain and the Corporate Junkie. Who, Where, Why and How?
- Conflicts and consideration in husband and wife businesses.
- General Hints and Suggestions for establishing a successful business.
- Extensive listing of organizations, networks and business resources.

THE ROLE OF MARKETING, PROMOTION, PUBLICITY AND ADVERTISING

As I write this book there are over one million people in this country who are worth over a million dollars and thousands upon thousands of people who are worth over ten million dollars. A great portion of this net worth is the equity in personal real estate, stocks and bonds, cash savings and many other valuable assets. If you consider the fact that there are at least fourteen million privately-owned businesses in the U.S., it would be pretty fair to say that business owners are likely to be well represented in this millionaire group.

A major reason why people get rich in business is obviously due to the fact that their businesses sell a lot of the product(s) or service(s) that they offer. The central question, the one everyone wants to know the answer to, is how do you get a lot of your product(s) or service(s) sold. This book, since it's about selling, might suggest that the best way for a business owner to increase sales is for him/her to learn how to sell better. This, however, is not the exact or total truth. You see, almost all wealthy business owners have directly removed themselves from actually selling their product(s) or service(s) to the customer.

Well, if this is the case, then you might assume that the successful business owner must have at least several excellent salespeople working for him/her. Well, yes, that is true also, but it is not the whole truth. The greater truth is that most of your wealthy business people have *sales-clerks* working for them. *Salesclerks!*, you may be thinking, isn't that what this book is trying to get away from. Salesclerks are a single step above vending machines. Why would an experienced salesperson start a business, take pride in his/her profession and end up using salesclerks when he/she reaches the pinnacle of financial glory. This situation and many others is what I will address in this section.

The Power of the Media

The expression, *the power of the media*, is a common one that people often hear with regard to the making of political events and figures, movie and television stars, criminals, diseases and any sort of controversy. But it is in the business world that media really has its most long-lasting impact. Business and media are a marriage that will never experience divorce. Many businesses would not have come into existence or have grown to the size they are today without the use of media. And virtually all media need to be paid by businesses in order to survive. In the last forty years the spectacular growth in sales of American (and foreign) products is much less due to a greater number of excellent salespeople as much as it has been the incredible impact of all forms of media. Within the last ten years particularly, the use and growth of media forms have been mind boggling. Let's look at it.

Television: Television, over the years, has made a steady impact as the screen got larger, reception improved and color was introduced. Within the last ten years, cable television has had a major impact on the nation. We've gone from a three network television audience to an audience that selects from up to thirty channels or more. Every one of these channels needs advertising dollars in one form or another and it is the business community that supplies theirs.

Magazines: Life magazine, Look magazine and the Saturday Evening Post were institutions in America in the middle decades of this century. One would think that with their death as regular weekly publications, "lesser" magazines would be in for an obvious struggle. Nothing could be further from the truth. Yes, it *is* a tremendous struggle for a magazine to survive in the 1980's, but there are many times more magazines that are making it today than ever before. Magazines cover virtually every topic you can think of, from baseball cards to hard-core pornography. In the health field, alone, there must be two dozen publications. Magazines exist because *businesses* have found it easier to reach their target market, in a cost effective way, by placing business ads in publications that relate closely to their product line. Without these business ad pages, *none* of these interesting magazines would exist.

Radio: About twenty-five years ago, almost every radio in America did not provide you the opportunity to listen to the FM band. The FM frequency was so underused that it just didn't make sense to build a radio to include something that virtually nobody would use. This idea might be very hard for a teenager today to understand. As a matter of fact, most adults probably have forgotten that fact. The growth of radio has been so spectacular that it has at least doubled, if not tripled, in the last two decades. How has this been possible? Very simply. Businesses have paid enough advertising money to support the existence of thousands of new radio stations. Without their dollars, the FM band would be as quiet now as it was twenty-five years ago.

Without providing additional examples at this time, the main point I want to make is that the power of the media has grown because there is more media, and as a result, the population has become more media dependent. Statistics say that if you combine radio, video, television, magazines, etc., people spend more time ingesting media messages than anything else. Embedded in all of these media sources are business messages. Supposedly, the average person absorbs about twenty-seven hundred advertisements, promotions, etc., *per day*.

The Introduction of Mass Marketing

Why, on the third Sunday in January, would a U.S. corporation spend a million dollars for a one-minute advertisement during the Super Bowl football game? And why would thousands of other corporations imitate this madness throughout the year? The reason is related to the concept of mass marketing. Mass marketing is the strategy of showing off a product to as large a population as possible with the idea that the more people who see it, the more people will inquire and/or buy it. Let me back up a second to explain in detail.

This book's purpose is to promote the idea of selling among a people who for various reasons have not generally participated in this enterprise.

That should be clear. Among the many topics covered in this book is the *selling* process, the process that professional salespeople are supposed to master. Within this process, I examined the concepts of prospecting (finding potential buyers), qualification (looking to see if the potential buyers fit the model, in terms of need and financial means) and presentation (demonstrating the product or service). After these expensive, time-consuming efforts, usually performed in front of one or more people at a time, the salesperson puts out his/her best effort for the purpose of making a sale. Sometimes he/she is successful, most times he/she not. Business owners who were looking for more efficient ways to sell their product(s) discovered and decided to use mass media. They figured that rather than having salespeople beat the pavements and the bushes for potential customers, they would use mass media to tell everybody about their product(s), with the assumption that the real hot customers will come to them. At that point all they have to do is take the customers' payment and pack up their goods. Is this concept new? Well, no, it's not. Eastern-based companies mailed catalogues and took ads in newspapers a hundred years ago and in so doing obtained customers in the Southern and Western parts of America. But through *television* and *national networks* with a *national viewing audience,* the concept of talking to millions of people at precisely the same time created a new advertising opportunity. Today, in the late 1980's, there is a good forty years of information on advertising compiled by thousands of very smart people. These people have spent billions and billions of dollars experimenting, refining, and testing ideas that have one fundamental purpose: To get a large number of people to buy a product or service immediately. Those companies that eventually became successful in getting a lot of people to buy their product(s) realized that they didn't need salespeople anymore, they needed *salesclerks*. Why? Because salespeople do prospecting, and that wasn't necessary anymore. Salespeople qualify prospects, and that wasn't necessary anymore. Salespeople go through demonstrations and use body language and study peoples' eyes, and that wasn't necessary anymore. Salespeople handle objections, but there were very few of those. The only thing that was really needed was a person to accept and count the money and put it into the cash register, and a clerk could do that. In addition to not needing the skills of a salesperson, business owners eliminated a lot of the cost of using salespeople (e.g., commissions, training, travel, etc.). A salesclerk costs almost nothing and come a dime a dozen: as soon as one leaves there are two or three to take his/her place.

The shining example of this type of business operation has always been McDonalds Restaurant. The entire sales transaction takes place sometimes in thirty seconds or less. No salespeople needed here. And within the last twenty years, most major retail establishments have adopted the instant service ideas of McDonalds. You have automobile tune-up shops, film processing centers, printing companies, pizza shops and a thousand other product companies that are all trying to be the "McDonalds" of their industry.

How does mass marketing work? Why is it so effective? How do business owners justify the high cost of mass marketing, wouldn't they be better off letting good salespeople do their job? We will look at the answer to these questions in a second. First, I have to define some words so that you can become familiar with the concepts.

Marketing: The broadest term used to described the process of selling something is the term marketing. Some say that *anything* connected to the sale of something is part of its marketing strategy. What the product is, what it is called, what size it is, where it is sold, how much it costs, etc., are all part of the marketing of the product. If an idea has anything to do with the product, from the time it is first thought up to the time it is in the hands of and paid for by the final customer, it is part of the marketing process.

Advertising: Advertising is one part of the marketing process. It is that portion of the process where the owner of the product *pays* another party to expose the product to the general public, usually for the purpose of selling it to them. Advertising is part of mass marketing in that the payment for exposure is being made because the product will be seen or heard by a very large number of people, a "massive" number of people.

Promotion: Promotion is that part of the marketing process which involves educating the public about the product in a persuasive way. More than just generally alerting the public to the existence of a product or service, promotion is designed to entice people to buy the product. Advertising is one form of promotion.

Publicity: It is often called free advertising. A feature story on a product as a news item in a magazine or on a television or radio program is publicity. It educates the public about a product, but it may or may not actually suggest or entice them to buy it. The review of a book, play, movie, record or painting is publicity. Free exposure.

P.R. or Public Relations: Public Relations is done by a public relations firm. These firms obtain, for a fee, publicity or "free" advertising for a company's product. The justification for paying for "free" media coverage is as follows. The fee you pay a firm may be lower than what you would pay an advertising firm to take out an ad, and the nature of your media coverage will be more extensive and more credible than a mere commercial ad.

Basic Theory of Mass Marketing

The basic theory in business is that all sales' cost something. People who buy things usually have a reason for buying X rather than Y. To get a customer into your building to buy your product takes some kind of investment. You have to invest in the building, the stocking of the product, the support staff and the equipment, all before the very first customer comes through the door. But customers don't automatically come through doors. Money has to be spent to get them in, and it costs money to get salespeople to the point where they can sell. Even after the sale, there is a cost that has to be paid to the salesperson for making the sale happen. If the customer paid by credit card, there is a cost to the owner for accepting the card. Everywhere the owner looks he/she sees expenses. Through sophisticated accounting and computer analysis, owners figure *a cost per sale*. Once that cost is known, much of the strategy of the businessperson is to reduce that cost. The three fundamental means used to get that cost figure down are as follows:

A. Let a greater number of people know about the product and get them into the store.

B. Once they are in the store, sell to a larger percentage of them.

C. Once they do buy the product, retain a larger portion of the profit for the business by reducing the amount paid out to the people who do the actual selling or the number of people who receive the money.

Mass marketing means making an all out pitch to the general population to come and look at your product. To market to the masses, however, you need mass media, something which captures the attention of tens or hundreds of thousands of people. Television, radio and publications can do this. Is it expensive? Well, yes and no. It it expensive if you look at the absolute figure in dollars and cents. But it may not be expensive if seen in cost per thousand of persons reached. Let me explain.

A person has a thousand dollars to spend to let people know about his/her grand opening. If flyers are printed up, he/she can get ten thousand done for a thousand dollars. But it takes fifteen hours of work to hand out those ten thousand flyers, and at a cost of four dollars an hour that comes to another sixty dollars. If an average of one and a half people see the flyers, that means that fifteen thousand people see the advertisement for one thousand sixty dollars spent. That comes to a cost of about seven cents per person reached.

If that person were to go to a newspaper, the ad person might say, "We will give you a full page ad and we have a circulation of sixty thousand readers." If half the readers notice the ad, then thirty thousand people will see the message, or twice the number of people reached through flyers. The cost per thousand of people reached goes from seven cents to three and a half cents.

If that person were to go to a television station, the ad person might say, "We will give you a thirty second mention during our midnight movie. We will have at least a hundred thousand people watching." Even if half get the message, that is fifty thousand people and your cost per thousand of people reached goes down to two cents per person.

This is a very simplified version of cost per thousand calculations, and there are many, many factors that have to be taken into consideration.

But the power of the media is a lot greater than just reaching more people. I have said, for the most part, that people are visual. Television can bring a product demonstration right into your home. You may pay more attention because it looks more exciting, more colorful, and more glamourous than if a pot-bellied salesman showed you the same thing down at the store. The announcer on the commercial may have such a commanding voice that it makes the product appear to be almost magical. Right there on the screen the product is compared to its competitor(s), and appears to be the clear winner in whatever comparison is being made. This selling situation does not provide a means for you to raise an objection because there is noone to object to; there is too little time to object; and, you aren't personally being pressured to buy at that exact moment. What you receive is one powerful, positive impact message. Another aspect about some media is that it can be and often is repeated. With every repetition you pick up a little more information, interest, curiosity, desire, etc.

People buy for both emotional and rational reasons. Good media presentations hit both parts of your brain. In effect, the product is often sold to the customer right there on the screen. All the customer has to do is to go down, pay for it and pick it up. He/she is sold. Mass media is effective because it is designed to do everything at once. It is geared to inform, stimulate emotions (pride, desire, etc.), demonstrate and tell exactly where to go to purchase the product.

Because mass media is effective, the cost is justified in the minds of many business owners. When they look at the cost of producing effective advertising and compare it to: a.) the number of new prospects, b.) the percentage of new prospects who buy as a result of advertising, and c.) the amount of money saved by replacing salespeople with salesclerks, it often means they get to keep more money by running the expensive ads. One of the greatest reasons in the world to do anything is that it works!

Marketing and Your Sales Career

Much of the information presented in this volume has been presented in broad terms. Naturally I have sought to make a distinction between mainstream reality and Black reality where appropriate. But I have not made very many distinctions between selling in a conservative, corporate setting, selling in a major, downtown department store and selling on the road in various towns within a given region. Then there is the distinction to be made between Black people who sell major manufacturers' products out of their own store versus Black people who sell their own product out of their own facility or on the road. It is all selling, true enough, but if we respect the concept of marketing, we know we have to consider every factor, from the product's development to its final sale to the consumer. Offered here now are some very general hints that you may want to consider.

a. Corporate Selling

If you are Black and sell for a Fortune 500 company, in all likelihood you are very much removed from the decisions on how to market the company's products. The decisions as to who the prime prospects are, how they are to be notified of the product, how they are to be approached, what to say, how to say it, etc., is probably already written up in the company training manual. Your job from the company's point of view is to learn it and do your job as well as the average White. Most large corporations don't seem to be very interested in creative techniques from new kids on the block, especially after they have spent hundreds of thousands, maybe millions of dollars, to research, develop and print the company training materials. You can learn a lot by studying how your company markets, promotes and advertises, and it will probably be information you can draw on at another point in your life. It has to help your sales career if you can understand and discuss the entire marketing philosophy of your company. If you know where the advertising is going, you can anticipate where the new prospects will be coming from, what their interests will be, and you will be that much better in your responses to them. On the other hand, if you see where you can make a contribution to redesigning marketing strategy as a result of your sales experience, that might help, too. Black Americans are not known for studying the *comprehensive* picture of the industries they are involved in. By being very clear on the entire spectrum of the marketing cycle, you will likely spot opportunities for yourself and position yourself for advancement within the company.

b. Local Retail Outlets

Much of what has been stated above would apply here, but there are some differences. Petty jealousy, seniority, personal politics, etc., may prevent many narrow-minded department store-type employees from appreciating input from a Black salesperson. On the other hand, many urban-based stores are looking for the Black employee who has a broad perspective to train as a manager as they seek to integrate the management of inner city operations. Perhaps that could be you. Another opportunity can be seen in the value of personal promotion and publicity. For example, let's say you sell refrigerators in an appliance store that is very popular within a particular community. You have five years experience and you are good and well liked. You have paid your dues, and you are a valuable asset to the store. At this point you can afford to stretch out, take some chances and risk going to the next step. What is the next step? The next step is to become a *media personality* or *character*. What is that? A media personality or character is someone who develops an identity, fame, or face recognition that is above and beyond what one would expect given what they do for a living. Examples might be "The Refrigerator" of the Chicago Bears, "Crazy Eddie", the popular stereo equipment dealer in New York, or "Doctor Ruth" of sex education fame. Of course, these are nationally known people and they have had much television exposure. But the same thing can be done on a local basis using local media, including radio and television. What do you have to do? Doing something a little different is the key. If you wear a funny suit or hat, talk a funny way (ever heard of Pee Wee Herman), take on selling challenges (breaking personal sales records, etc.) or otherwise do something unique, you might draw an unusual amount of attention to yourself. Of course you have to "feel" this role enough to be believable, and of course you would have to clear the idea with your supervisor. You will also need to draw up a complete plan of how you are going to promote yourself at least a year in advance so that you don't appear to be a one-shot publicity stunt. Then do it with *commitment*. Your sales should rise if for no other reason than people like to be in the company of news-makers, oddities and successful people, even those they know are manufactured (ever see adults on Santa Clause's lap). Can you see how this might go over at an appliance store but not at IBM?

c. Self-Employed Black Salespeople Selling National Brands

These people have three marketing options that are all legitimate ways to sell. First, they can play it *straight*. They can consult with their national brand product representatives and follow the marketing plan as outlined. They can develop one of those kinds of stores where people say, "Oh, I didn't know this place was Black-owned. If someone hadn't told me I would have never known." (Note: To some people this *is* success; to be so un-Black is the highest stage of perfection). Here the owner would more than likely serve a predomi-nately White clientele and subscribe to the more conservative set of business practices.

The second option is to start your enterprise off in some alter ego style. The term "Doctor" has become popular ever since Dr. J. made his impact in basketball. I've seen the Credit Doctor (sells furniture), the Auto Doctor, another Credit Doctor (repairs personal credit), the Washer Doctor (repairs washing machines), etc. Being a character is not easy and it may interfere with aspects of your personal life. But poverty and bankruptcy may interfere with your personal life also, and if the *personalization* of your business can prevent that, you may want to consider it.

The third option is to simply combine the two over a period of time. You might want to start straight, play by all the rules, and when you think it's safe, and you have established a degree of professionalism and follow through, then go for broke to get wealthy.

Self-employed Black Salespeople Selling Their Own Products and/or Services

Of all the people in the spectrum examined here, the self-employed black salesperson selling his/her own product needs the most marketing assistance. The first question to be asked and addressed is, What part of the total consumer market do you claim as "yours" (your prime prospects) and why? I have said that people buy more on emotion than reason. If your claim of a market niche is based solely on the *logic* of people "naturally" wanting your product to fill a need (a need *you* assume they have), your marketing plan may already be in trouble. What is it that you offer that is different enough to encourage people to leave where they are going right now to come to you? If they were to brag about or refer your business to others, what would be the obvious thing that they would mention *besides* the fact that you are Black? Are you counting on support just because you are Black? How much competition do you have and can the market support all of you?

After you are convinced that you know who your customers are, you have to identify how customers are to know about you. This is the single, most crucial step for the success of new Black businesses - it is called promotion. It won't do you much good to have good products at good prices and extensive experience in selling if you don't have customers to serve. What precisely do you promote? I have heard a lot of jive talk from people in business, getting ready to go into business or thinking about starting a business. Over the years what I have learned to do is to listen for *a specific reason to take them seriously*. I mention that because right now no group of people in America has a lower level of respect in the area of business than Black people. Basketball, yes, or boxing, or baseball, but not business. Thus, when we announce to the world that we are opening a business, there is no response to speak of from either the Black or White communities. People have learned not to get their hopes up, and they take a wait and see attitude. Many more people can open a business than can actually run one. Thus, if you are Black, you need a reason to be taken seriously, by everybody. That reason could be anything. It could be the physical attractiveness of the business itself, the amount of inventory you have on hand, its location, your low or high sale prices, your fine quality of goods, your experienced background, or anything that might suggest "this one might be different, they can't all fail." Whatever the most serious aspect of your business, whatever the single best reason for people to take the whole enterprise seriously, *promote that idea or characteristic, heavily.* After that point, you should be consistent. In the world of business, Black folks' basic tendency is inconsistency in almost everything, from the amount of inventory to the operating hours to whether telephone calls get returned. The two things a new businessperson needs to make sure they are consistent about is promotion and re-investment back into the business. People, Black and White, expect you to start off with a bang and limp along until you collapse. It has happened thousands of times. It's not that they are negative or unsupportive (although this can very well be the case), it's just that they are very experienced observers and they know what they have seen. If a person doesn't study business, particularly selling and promotion, aren't they bound to repeat the same mistakes over and over again?

How do you promote your business? It is not likely that a new Black business will have much in the way of advertising dollars. Even if you did, it would probably be more cost effective to get publicity (free advertising) rather than take out expensive ads. A new business needs credibility even more than exposure. Publicity can generate credibility and/or curiosity better than ads because a third party is commenting and making "objective" observations. General media publicity doesn't always extend free coverage to all new enterprises just because they are new. There must be a "hook", something unusual enough to get a significant number of somebodies to stop and take notice in the paper, magazine, or on television. Hopefully, your reason to be taken seriously is unique enough, controversial enough or strong enough to merit media coverage. Other inexpensive ways to cultivate a customer base include:

a. Personal letters: Computer printers can crank out a copy of a letter that looks extremely impressive. Change the heading to make each one personal. This letter is to alert all potentially interested parties. Surprisingly a well-written, well-spaced letter will get the attention of even busy people. State that you will follow-up with a phone call at a certain time and then do it. This helps establish confidence in your ability to follow through.

b. Telephone: Time consuming but personal. Write out your script first, or at least an outline, and be professional, not mechanical.

c. Free seminars and demonstrations: Offer your expertise free as an introduction to your profit-making business. Give people a chance to sample you or your product(s) and service(s). You will learn a lot the first few times you try it in any event. You'll discover where your prospects are really coming from; it might not be from where you first imagined. You'll learn what people want from you if you aren't offering the product or service now. Find out how your pricing structure strikes them during some candid give and take conversation. Develop a mailing list for future use. Record yourself for presentation study. A free seminar should be a test run for the absolute novice, and a practice or work session for the more experienced presenter.

d. Local trade shows, conventions and large gatherings: The benefits of setting up a display table at a large gathering are similar to the ones listed above. Hopefully, the opportunity to actually sell your product or service will present itself. Trade shows have a way of making new businesspeople more realistic with regard to the appeal of their products and the types and percentages of people who are *really* interested. Trade show gatherings provide tremendous opportunities for you to observe the merits of various competitors' products and watch consumer response to them. You should build your personal network through contacts made at trade shows, and perhaps decide to add or subtract items from your own product line. You will learn how to display and promote by watching others perform. If you are in a new city, make sure you use the yellow pages to contact potential retailers of your product. In this way you build your distribution system through in-person dealings, and, hopefully you will leave that town with up-front payments if you have a unique product not readily available in that local area.

e. Promotional items - pens, tee shirts, bumper stickers: If you've made up your mind to promote a particular product or line of products for the long term, you ought to consider obtaining promotional items. You must realize that a lot of buying is based on curiosity, or rather the satisfaction of it. People are always saying, "I just want to try it." I can think of nothing more valuable in raising curiosity than a well-stated bumper sticker. Even if you had just two hundred riding on the bumpers of cars in an average town, do you know how much exposure that would be for such a small amount of money? I don't know about you but I almost feel compelled to read a sticker when I approach a car at a light or even when I'm riding down the highway. Most are designed to be funny. If you design yours to arouse curiosity and people keep reading them every week all over town, I can almost guarantee that people will visit your business just to satisfy their building interest and curiosity. At that point the ball is in your court.

f. Collective efforts - Black Pages: As more Black businesses struggle for survival, it doesn't take folks long to see the futility of reinventing the wheel. In many cities a listing of all Black-owned businesses exists and it is usually called the Black Pages. Much smaller groups sponsor mail-order brochures together or do other collective marketing ventures.

g. Newsletter publishing: A major problem that will plague you, as it does other Black businesspeople, is the assumption that your products, knowledge, experience and contacts are inferior. This, very often, will not be stated directly to you, so you can't address what can't be seen or heard. Or can you? Producing a good newsletter should put to rest many of the doubts that others may have about you. But in the case of newsletters you are demonstrating your expertise in a positive way, not coming from a defensive posture. In your newsletter you groom your audience for a future purchase with notices about things you are about to do or produce. You may offset the cost of producing the document by taking in some advertising from others, thereby increasing, in a public way, your base of supporters and believers.

h. Periodically offer a good sale item: Black folks expect a "break" from other Black businesses because they confuse what little business knowledge they may have with our sociological experiences, and they come out with their own theories. As any Black businessperson knows, we have more problems to overcome than the majority population, not less. We are in the weakest economic position. We are also in the weakest position to offer freebies or lost leaders. But in actual practice, it probably proves to your valuable supporters that you are not always out to make a buck off of them if you offer of a good sale item once in a while.

Summary

Salespeople need to master their craft to ensure good incomes from their profession. But many companies are moving away from depending on salespeople to do good jobs to realize their profits. Through the use of highly sophisticated marketing strategies, many companies are using the media to convince consumers to just come down and pick up their products after payment. The only demonstration presentation they need to note is the one they see on the screen. After McDonalds set the tone for instant consumer gratification, many other companies and industries have followed suit. This idea tends to somewhat threaten the stability of professional salespeople in certain industries. It behooves salespeople to study the marketing plan of their companies, either to sell better or to read the signs of change. Knowledgeable salespeople can contribute to the development of marketing strategies for their employers or they can start their own companies and be responsible for their own marketing strategies. Some Blacks have a choice as to how they market themselves and their businesses. They can either play it straight or come up with a gimmick or ongoing publicity generator to promote sales. Independent Black entrepreneurs moving their own products need to give the public, and certainly their prospects, a reason to be taken seriously. They need to constantly promote themselves and their product(s) in a cost effective way and use the profits from the enterprise to improve the business. A record of consistency is needed for both the image and profitability of Black businesses. You must understand that selling techniques, the very thing you are just coming to understand, has taken a backseat to today's promotional power because it pushes the sales figures along a lot faster. New Black businesspeople must put the needs of their businesses above their own if they expect to succeed as business owners. We live in a nation exploding with ambitious, entrepreneurial types who are of all colors, and who enter the game more experienced, better connected and generally more resourceful.

BACK TO
BASIC BLACK

Up to this point I have given you some selling fundamentals which I believe to be fairly accurate and complete. In a perfect world they would be all you'd need to get started. You, the reader, must absorb these concepts and apply and adapt them to your particular personality, product line and market. This is what any author of a similar book would tell you to do, because we are all unique individuals with a unique personal history, set of goals and expectations. But it is more than your unique personality that will call for you to adopt these principles in a certain way. Your Blackness in the business world will have an impact as great as almost any other aspect of your being. Your Blackness will have a huge affect on how people, Black and White, react to you and what they will expect of you. Possibly the worse mistake you can make as a Black salesperson, in my opinion, is to assume or pretend that your Blackness will have no affect one way or another on your selling career. You will not begin your sales career with a totally blank sheet of paper on which you'll inscribe only those impressions and messages that you intend to send out to the world. No, there is already writing on the wall about you because you are Black. There are millions of people who think that they already know a lot about you because you are Black. They have prejudged you, and what you say and do will simply be added to the impression that they already have about you (and anyone else who is Black). Many of the people who have prejudged you are themselves Black, and rightly or wrongly they will assume that your values, strengths and weaknesses are like their own. So the reality is that you really have at least two tasks. You must first learn about the art, the profession, the world of selling. And secondly, if you are to maximize your effectiveness, you must come to understand and act on what it means to be a *Black* salesperson. These two challenges are very interrelated but can sometimes be at odds with *one another*, as you will learn soon enough.

The Role of Self-Image

You have heard the expression that a chain is only as strong as its weakest link. I want to relate that idea to the concept of Black Americans selling goods and services.

Many Blacks can choose an excellent product to sell, develop a strong belief in the product, have an attractive price and minimal competition, and still fail miserably in sales. Why? Because in spite of all these strong chain links, the weak link is often that Black person's concept of him/herself. He/she has a low sense of self-worth and a poor self-image. If you lack confidence, pride and a love of yourself, you will project a hesitant, clumsy, insecure image. What you say will not be believed and you will fail. This is a big part of what plagues the Black community. White America's feeling of self-worth is so high that all around the world they are known to be cocky and arrogant. Racism in fact helps White America feel superior to all other people of the world. You must never forget that racism exists because it benefits (in a limited way) the people who believe in it. If *everybody* thought racism served no purpose, it would disappear like small pox.

But just as racism helps the feeling of self-worth among many Whites, it weakens the feeling of self-worth among Blacks. The projection of powerful images in the media and throughout society of the slow, unintelligent Black person gives most Blacks a strong reason for doubting their abilities and potential. Many Blacks are willing and able to fight these stereotypical images by learning to speak so-called "proper English", by "dressing for success", by graduating from the right (White) colleges, and by mastering technical subject matter. But the fight against stereotypical images becomes a problem itself when, to dispel the "typical Black image" Black folk struggle to become something they are not.

Many of these "right moves" are simply weak imitations of White mannerisms, and they lack personal meaning to the Blacks making them. Many of these Blacks work in job environments where "everybody is phony" and most employees simply learn to tolerate everyone else's degree of phoniness. As a Black phony the situation is not all that threatening. As a matter of fact many Blacks welcome this type of environment (often called a "sophisticated" environment) *because* they can cover up their feelings of self-hate and insecurity by playing a phony role. It is *easier* for them to act like someone else rather than be themselves because of their poor self-image. If they are successful in playing the role, they are admitted into the in-crowd as a bonafide member in good standing with all the rights and privileges thereof. Over time, however, even many of these Black folk tire of the game and develop a worse self-image *because* they realize that so much of what they do is unreal, and they have begun to feel guilty about it.

In the sales situation (which is to say the entrepreneurial situation) things are very different. Your sales will not be based on the school you attended, how you dress, what clubs you belong to, etc. While these things may occasionally bear upon a specific situation, the true test in selling is your persuasion skills and degree of believability. Phoniness in the long run will kill a sales and business career. Sales' tests, unlike college tests or tests for a promotion, do not involve information that you can forget one week after the test. In sales you are tested and challenged every working hour. If you pass, you eat. If you fail, you are broke. Nothing can be more real than that. To put yourself in this kind of environment on a daily basis you must feel good about yourself and your abilities. You must understand and like people, which would be impossible if you did not understand and like yourself. And this must be confirmed in reality by your success in relating to people to the extent that they are willing to give you their hard earned and limited money in exchange for what you are selling.

As a salesperson it is not your job to prove to each client that his/her prejudgments of you are right or wrong. You want to respond to prospects but not be forced to react to or be controlled by them. *You* are in control. You want to help them make the proper purchasing decision. You will do this to the best of your ability unless their prejudice proves to you, without question, that they do not appreciate or want your expert advice. At that time you will then tactfully remove yourself from that unproductive situation and take your valuable time and skills to one that's more promising.

Improving Your Self-Image

It is not enough to simply state the facts as they usually are, we must understand how to make changes. How do we get Black folks to feel better about themselves, thus developing more potential to be better salespeople? This is the million dollar question that thousands of people much brighter than I have been trying to solve for decades. Frederick Douglas, W.E.B. Dubois, Carter G. Woodson (particularly in *The Miseducation of The Negro)*, the honorable Elijah Muhammad, and many others have all tried to project a more positive image of the African-American personality, but they've had mixed results. I offer here some ideas to be added to the vast body of information already produced to change the African-American outlook and perspective.

a. The self-image *can* be changed: All of us have seen *proof* that an individual can change his/her physical appearance by following a particular diet and/or exercise routine. We have seen skinny people become fat, fat people become thin, and fat and skinny people become muscular. We have seen plastic surgery, for better or worse, change the way people look. In short, we know that people can physically change, and certainly the physical self is a significant part of one's self-image. We have seen people fall in love, have children, turn to God, lose a mother, father or relative and *change* their *feelings and emotions* about the world, people, relationships, themselves and the unknown. We know that feelings can and do change, and that ones feelings are a large part of his/her self-image. So if one's body, emotions and spiritual feelings can change and they all interrelate to one's image of oneself, then ones self-image can change. This might sound like an elementary point, but people have to be thoroughly convinced that something is possible before they attempt to do it.

Many Blacks feel that their opinion of themselves is set and static for life. If they are fat, poor, unattractive, low in energy, susceptible to sickness, disliked etc, they feel that "that is the way things were meant to be." "That it's Gods will." "That it's reality." Our first step, then, is to say with conviction that self-image can be changed and improved.

b. Active blueprinting: Your self-image is to your actions and your life what a blueprint is to a building. Just as a contractor constructs a building according to the blueprint, so to a person's actions, ideas, habits and speech follows his/her self-image. Altering a few lines and numbers on a single sheet of paper (blueprint), could change how an entire skyscraper would eventually looks. In that same vein, altering self-image, could change the actions, responses, looks, communication patterns and eventually the entire direction of one's life. What is needed by most people, after they understand and believe in the value and possibility of changing (improving) their self-image, is the will and a plan to actually do so. I call the plan to change self-image *active blueprints*. Active blueprints require you to design and measure your goals and dreams.

If you are like most people, Black and White, you are simply a collection of pieces of advice from dozens of people. Your parents, teachers, ministers, peers, coaches, work supervisors, and mates have all thrown hundreds of millions of words and advice at you over the years. If you add in a few thousand hours of television, movies and magazines, well, here you are. What I am saying is that you are an accident. You could just as easily have been a very different person if you had different teachers, peers, mates, magazines, etc. You probably did not control the type of information coming into your brain. If you are to *actively blueprint* your life, you must *sit down and write out a redesigned you.*

You must decide on the *intellectual you* - what you want to know and how you will go about learning it.

You must decide on the *physical you* - what you want to look like and how you will attain that look.

You must decide on the *financial you* - how much money you want to have and how that money will come to you.

You must likewise design yourself as a spiritual person, social person, parent person, mate-lover person, etc. Then you must digest as much information and perform as many actions as you can to achieve your goals. You cannot write out a blueprint and never look at it again. You must compare your actions against your blueprint every day to make sure they are in line. When you have your blueprint etched into your brain, then you will have effectively changed your self-image. When you have seen some of your goals and challenges met and surpassed, you will have given reinforcement to all the theories and beliefs that preceeded it.

But personal blueprinting and personal self-images are not enough. Black people see themselves and are seen by others as a group. We cannot and should not want to escape that. Instead as we improve ourselves individually, we must never forget to relate to the group. We need to be a resource for Black America as a whole, we need to give it our strength and be able to utilize its strength when we go through periods of weakness. Our quest for success should not just be for ourselves or even our families, but for the family of Black America and the family of man. Does this sound idealistic and like so much rhetoric? Maybe. But see how long you stay committed, disciplined and consistent if all it's really about is just you. You will make excuses for *you.* Will you be as likely to make as many excuses for your lack of development if you know that your children's, grandchildren's and your community's future is riding on your efforts? People even *die sooner* when they live alone and for only themselves.

The Sales Process - Black and White Contrasts

Selling Formats

Even before I explore the differences in styles between selling to the White and Black communities, you must see that even the selling formats can pose problems.

1. *Direct and Multi-Level Sales*:

The Black community, having a substantial inferiority complex, will often buy an item more for prestige than functional purpose. Blacks are very name brand, style and status conscious. Very few direct or multi-level companies can offer these characteristics and thus a disproportionate number of Blacks may refuse to purchase very good products for no sound reason. If a name brand item is serving them well and they feel better about themselves because they can afford the highly advertised (and supposedly most desired) product, they have little to gain by switching to an unknown product that "isn't good enough for the stores."

Also, in direct and multi-level selling the salesperson supposedly offers his/her "personal service" and "convenience" along with the product that he/she sells. However, the *experience* of many Black people who buy from a Black salesperson is that he/she quickly breaks appointments and promises of delivery (no different from carpenters, plumbers or electricians, really), or he/she is very late, and therefore *inconvenient* for them. Because the turnover in direct sales companies is so high, the salesperson may have quit the business by the time the customer is ready to reorder. And often a new salesperson, due to limited finances or inexperience, may not have nearly enough stock for the customer to select from when he/she is ready to purchase. Consequently, what was originally "sold" as *convenience* often becomes a source of *frustration* and *inconvenience*. When people go through this situation once or twice, they tend to shy away from becoming customers again. Thus if you are starting to sell through this mode, you will have to pay for the problems and frustrations caused by people who preceded you. If you continue the same jive, then the cycle will remain intact.

In terms of building a sales organization, there can be (though not necessarily) problems with Blacks and Whites. Black folks, who are still relatively new to sales, are still hesitant, for the most part, for all the reasons mentioned earlier. To build a strong, stable sales organization that is principally Black in makeup is almost like expecting new Asian and South American immigrants to be drafted into the N.B.A. It is outside the current cultural patterns of both groups. For Black Americans, however, it *is* our current challenge. Like every generation we have the responsibility of doing and confronting things that other generations did not do or did not have to confront. One of the ways that Black America will develop great salespeople is to involve nearly everyone in a concrete sales program so that potentially poor salespeople can seek other careers, and the potentially good salespeople can be identified, encouraged and allowed to rise to the top. That's the way it works today in basketball in our community. Now we have to begin the tradition in sales.

Another factor that affects Blacks in building strong sales organizations is the reluctance on the part of both Blacks and Whites to follow Black leadership. Even when a good Black salesperson emerges, people have difficulty trusting him/her. Blacks shy away because of ego problems and/or jealousy. Interested Whites may shy away simply because they are not used to following Blacks in anything. Even in sports Whites are the owners, lawyers, judges, referees, officials, agents and coaches, and they call all the *real* shots. Most Whites have a real problem asking their friends and family to follow a Black leader, even if they are fair minded themselves. When Whites learn about a good opportunity from a Black, they will usually get all the pertinent information and then seek to follow someone whom they feel more "comfortable" with or who "lives in their area."

2. Mail-Order Sales:

There are thousands upon thousands of different mailing lists which can be rented by anyone who wishes to do so. Virtually all of these lists are composed of White Americans. If you as a salesperson had a product or service that you wanted to offer to the nation's Black community, you would probably find all of about ten lists of Black Americans of the twenty thousand or so that exist. And once you did locate a list you would probably find that at least twice as many of your flyers would be returned to you as would be the case if you sent materials to White prospects. Why would this happen? Because a higher percentage of Whites live in property that they own (houses, townhouses, condominiums, co-ops, etc.) than Black folks, and they are more permanently anchored in their communities. When Whites do move they make a point to give their change of address to the Post Office, because they are not running away from bill collectors, irate landlords, and the like. And, finally, even though credit cards and eight hundred telephone numbers are so much a part of today's buying, you will find Blacks less likely to use them because many do not have credit or they are over extended on their credit cards. Do Whites have all the problems that I am listing for Blacks? Of course they do, but as always it is a matter of degree and numbers. Black people are, numerically speaking, a minority in this country. A smaller part of this minority has more discretionary income to buy certain items than the larger population. If this same group moves more often and is less likely to use credit cards, one ought to be able to see the difficulty in capturing this market.

There are of course many Black professional organizations that have extensive mailing lists. The National NAACP has over four hundred thousand members. The National Baptist Convention has over a million. Ebony magazine has over a million subscribers listed in its computer. But these organizations and publications guard their members like a hen watches over her chicks. The only way to get to their members is to advertise in their publications, period. Although there is a lot of lip service given to the idea of "sharing resources", the reality is that virtually everyone jealously guards his/her turf and constituents. Even new, Black networking groups judiciously guard the addresses of their one hundred or so members (sometimes even from themselves) to protect the members from an "unwanted invasion of privacy." Black entrepreneurs suffer from these policies. They cannot easily reach by mail the Black "upscale market."

Blacks wishing to sell goods to other Blacks by mail usually encounter two other problems. Many sellers, for whatever reason, legitimate or not, do not offer a money-back guarantee with the purchase. Many folks will not send money through the mail without this understanding. And secondly, Blacks do not yet manufacture much of what they sell, so they have a limited profit percentage mark-up. When you note the expenses involved in mail-order copy, printing, postage, labor, fulfillment costs, etc., and combine them with limited lists and all the problems mentioned previously, you can see how difficult a business venture this can be for the Black entrepreneur serving the Black Market.

Prospecting and Referrals

Above I discussed the difficulty in identifying a large, stable pool of Black prospects from which a salesperson could consistently draw. Fortunately, there are many networking groups in large cities that one can utilize to collect business cards and build contact lists. The difference between Black and White networking groups is that White groups have a much higher percentage of self-employed people who can sell their services as professionals. Black networking groups have a higher number of people who hand out cards showing where they work (as employees), and their duties limit in many ways the assistance they can offer people outside of their employment structure. The purpose of many Black networking sessions is to get leads to *new jobs* for the participants rather than to buy from or sell to Black salespeople and businesspeople.

For referrals it is almost mandatory for Blacks to pay some type of referral fee to those who refer purchasing customers to them. There are several reasons for this. First, with respect to White customers, I can only repeat what was stated earlier. There are situations where a liberal thinking White person may be completely open to accepting Blacks, Asians, Hispanics, homosexuals and women in authoritative positions. But this liberal person might be more liberal than his/her friends and family members. So rather than offending them, or having to hear some unnecessary static or argument for referring an "undesirable", that liberal person might not bother to make a referral at all. But with the economic incentive of a discount on a future purchase or a cash payment, he/she may refer someone to you.

In Black folks' eyes, referrals work against one of the main reasons for buying unique and exclusive products. Why, for example, should a woman who has purchased a particular fur coat, piece of jewelry, or a furniture setting for the purpose of "showing off" to her friends and family, refer these same people to the source of her purchase? If a person found out that a half dozen of his/her friends purchased the same or similar products that he/she did, then the purchase would be considered "no big thing" and it would lose alot of its appeal to everyone. I'm sure you have heard about or know women who have gone to an affair and felt crushed because someone else had on the same outfit that they did. I can't, however, imagine a person not referring a good computer or encyclopedia salesperson to you for fear that you might buy the same computer or encyclopedia set. In any event, a referral fee might make many people reveal their "secret" sources.

Another reason a Black salesperson is likely to have to offer a financial incentive for referrals is because Blacks have a long history of feeling used. Black folks can see very plainly how all kinds of people are making money from them personally and as a community in general. Somehow when people with profitable enterprises are *not* Black the situation is tolerated because Blacks feel they are powerless against the unified actions of other groups. They submit to the unified power and organization of other ethnic groups. Jews, Italians, Koreans, Cubans, Japanese, Vietnamese, and others are not perceived by Blacks as individuals, but as part of a force that is futile to fight or complete against. Then along comes a Black salesperson who asks Blacks to refer other Blacks so that he/she can make more money. Black consumers at this point, *do not* see the Black salesperson as an oncoming force over whom they have no control and to whom they have to submit; the person is Black and they know that there is no unified Black economic force. Black consumers see an individual: isolated, struggling and vulnerable. An individual who also happens to be Black. They see someone who they feel should be willing to negotiate, and compromise. Why should they help this struggling individual make more money? Why should they (from their twisted points of view) knowingly and willingly contribute to their own feelings of inadequacy by supporting someone whom they believe is no better than themselves. No, if a Black consumer is to help a weak, Black salesperson (a weak Black salesperson is perceived by the Black consumer as someone who, for the most part, has to have local Black consumers, because that's just about his/her only hope for a customer base) he/she must get something for it. Otherwise, the consumer feels used by *everybody*. In many Black peoples' minds, if you have been used by other Blacks then you have effectively been used by *everybody*. To many Blacks, being used is when they help another person make money (through a referral perhaps) and get nothing of value in return. Looked at in one way, it is a very sad and sick way of reasoning. But looking at it another way, it means that even the poor Black on the street knows that people are only suppose to submit (if that is what they think they are doing) *to power* and it is not something that Blacks have been able to harness in the economic arena. In other words, many Blacks do not respect Blackness but they have common sense enough to respect real power. And in their minds, when Blackness *stands* for real economic power and they are *made* to respect it, they will, but not before.

The best way for Blacks to get prospects seems to be through personal promotion, which will be covered shortly.

Qualifying of Prospects

In most instances a person does not have to be "qualified" to purchase everyday items. But for items that are expensive or require financing, the Black salesperson could find themselves in a very delicate situation because he/she often has to ask some rather personal questions.

In the case of interviewing typical White prospects, some may be resentful that a Black individual, who in their minds has only recently been liberated, could be in position to determine if *they* (White people) are qualified for anything. Most people get a little uptight about revealing their real income, debts, assets, credit and the like; but, to do so with a person who is not considered one's equal may be really pushing past the point of reason. Contributing to this hesitancy is the fact that if a Black person has the authority to *ask* these questions, then he/she could quite possibly have the authority to *deny* worthiness, and for some that would be rather hard to stomach. It would be adding insult to injury. In these cases, tactfulness and a high degree of diplomacy are of utmost importance. In problem situations it may be in the best financial interest of the Black salesperson to have a White third party obtain the needed information.

In the case of a Black buyer, a Black salesperson may have a slightly different problem. The Black consumer, as an individual, has been constantly questioned, harassed and required to prove qualifications all of his/her life. Many of these hassles had a racial basis. Now they come to a Black-owned store and are asked the same temperature-raising questions by a Black person that racist Whites have been asking for years. Part of the cause of this frustration is that Black folks are not taught the ins and outs of credit and money system in the first place. They do not understand the kind of protection that banks, companies and owners need to prevent the wholesale loss of goods and income. Thus, every time these uninformed consumers are asked the standard questions, they consider it a personal attack on their integrity and a reminder of past wrongs committed by other people at other places. Unfortunately, the Black salesperson may have to take the loss because often these angry consumers storm out of the buying site convinced that "Black business folks are just as bad as the White ones." Until the so-called educators in the Black community educate our people about finances, these situations will occur over and over again for years to come, and Black salespeople and the Black economy will suffer because of it.

Presentation Skills

It was stated earlier that a good product presentation starts with a good presentation of the salesperson. It was also mentioned earlier that a person should be mindful of his/her dress, body odors, grooming, etc. As important as these things are, it must be made clear that regardless of the care you give to your attire, the very first thing a customer will notice is that you are Black. That will register just before or just after they notice you are a male or female. Thus, if you are in the business arena and you habitually deal with people who respect Blacks as people but not as business people, you have a bit of a problem. Millions of salespeople who have been told *"don't take rejection personally"* move on to the next customer without missing a beat. That might work to settle the shaken confidence of a White salesperson. But when you are Black and look dead into the blue eyes of another human being and those eyes say, "I don't trust you because you are what you are", you can't help but take it rather personally because your race is definitely a part of you. How do you deal with it? You proceed anyway and accept it as a personal challenge. How did little children deal with desegregating schools? How did Jackie Robinson deal with baseball or Jessie Owens deal with Hitler? Businesspeople have to be fighters, and without question Black businesspeople have to be fighters. They are fighting both for and against. They are fighting for a piece of their community's economic pie. They are fighting for the development of higher standards among Black businesspeople. But they are also fighting against the notion that Black people cannot do business like other people, that they can't sell and that they can't negotiate and compromise to their economic benefit with people they haven't always been friendly towards.

Some prospects and customers may not like you on first impression. So what, sometimes you start in the hole. You have the power of your voice, words, facial expressions, body language, intelligence, persuasion skills, appearance, gender, eye contact and other resources yet undeveloped to turn this prospect's mind around. And in so doing you may do what young boys do on the playground. You remember, don't you? You battle the bully and, win or lose, you gain his respect. Latter you may develop a weird sort of friendship based on this respect. With enough friends, the bully stops having the need to be a bully.

When a Black person "sells" a racist or a conservative, he/she is winning the battle of *silver rights*, the battle we are engaged in right now. One way to ensure that we lose this crucial battle (and the whole war against poverty that was started over twenty years ago) is not to participate in the fight. The rules haven't changed much in twenty years either. Namely, if you are not part of the solution (out there selling something), you very well could be part of the problem.

With regard to the presentation of products to a Black market, it must be kept in mind that a huge amount of the advertising and promotional dollars in this country are not directed towards the Black market. Thus, a Black salesperson should not assume that just because the average White prospect is familiar with his/her company or its products that the average Black prospect will be also. Black America is part of America but it is usually forced to live in a community of its own. And in that community certain messages never get in *its* newspapers, magazines, billboards and other advertising media. Thus, the Black salesperson has to be aware that he/she is not merely familiarizing or demonstrating a product or service to some Black prospects, he/she may be making a first time introduction of that product or service. And let's be honest, it is difficult for a person to be introduced to a product and be expected to buy it on that same day: especially if it is an item of significant cost and specialized use. Yet if Black salespeople do not take the responsibility to introduce new products to our community, our only other option is to wait for the White community to determine us to be "ready", which might be never. Not only would this hurt the Black community, it would be a big loss to Black salespeople in some instances. Who, more than the people that stimulate, educate and develop a market, deserves to make a win-fall profit from the sale of a new product. This then is both the up and the down side of being a Black salesperson. You must cultivate your community like a farmer cultivates a field of crops. You must tend to it, care for it and make sure you are around when the harvest arrives. It is hard and tedious work, but one good harvest, and you, your children and maybe your grandchildren could be set for life. It happens all the time, with the other people.

Responding To Objections

Sometimes people do things and they do not know why they did them. They are often unable to recapture the state of mind which made them turn left when everything pointed towards making a right turn. It's called instinctive or spontaneous response, and if a customer gives you a rejection yet does not know why he/she is doing it, it is hard to feel perfectly confident that you know why either. Part of the power of racism is that *it is* so instinctive and automatic that people who respond for racist reasons are not aware or deny to themselves that it is or was a factor in their thinking. Black salespeople however, have the sensitive antennae that pick up the racist vibe even when prospects are unaware their signal is being transmitted.

Much is said in sales literature about trust and its role in making a sale happen. Everyone wants to be sure that he/she trusts all aspects of a transaction before handing over his/her money. He/she wants to trust the product, the manufacturer, the retailer and the salesperson. The salesperson is the real key because he/she is the only live person the customer interacts with. The manufacturer is usually in another county, and the product is wrapped in instructions and warnings which have to be read and studied. The retailer is a large chain where any real authority figure is in a home office somewhere a hundred miles away. So it comes down to the salesperson. The customer must have faith in the salesperson and that faith must be based on something. That faith is based on the customer's belief that the salesperson is not just honest but also understands his/her problems, needs, resources and limitations, and that all these issues don't have to be spelled out during the transaction. This is a strong case for why people *naturally* buy from someone who is like themselves and of the same community. The words and assumptions in the communication mean the same thing to each of them. But perhaps you are a Black salesperson in a mostly White industry. From the point of view of White prospects, is it reasonable for them to assume that you *do know* them and their problems, needs, resources and limitations without them having to spell it all out. In truth I think you would have to admit there is no basis for them to assume that, especially if you are of a different sex, age and race. So what I am saying is that, even in the best of circumstances, there does appear to be rather objective reasons why race does sometimes make a difference (as does sex, age, social class, etc.) in terms of the comfort that one person may want to experience to buying from another. Of course, this would apply more to buying a yacht than buying a can of sardines.

What I am saying then is that racism alone will cause objections to arise when there is no other basis for one. Usually the prospect doesn't even know why he/she is objecting, but "it doesn't feel right", or "something is missing." As a Black salesperson you have to be calm in reacting to this situation. You can't blame people for being products of their environment (the United States of America), nor will you get anywhere by even suggesting that they are objecting because you are Black. You have to out finesse them, smooth them over and get them sold. This is where market knowledge comes in. If you know your product but do not know the various profiles of the people who buy your product, then yes, you *are* a stranger. But if you've got on a suit and tie, and you can talk about the concerns and lifestyles of your market to the extent that they see that you do know something about their interests, experiences, goals, etc., then you can cut down on the social distance that makes the buyer uncomfortable about buying. If you can address his/her specific concerns then you will become more believable and worthy of trust.

The prejudice of Black consumers towards Black salespeople has some basis in fact and experience, whether we feel comfortable about admitting it or not. Although there is still the cry against KKK violence, trigger happy police and segregated jury boxes, the greater cry today is against Black-on-Black crime fueled by drugs, poor leadership, self-hatred and miseducation. Much of the loss of property and income that many Blacks have experienced, particularly in Northern urban centers, has been at the hands of other Blacks. If selling is a matter of communicating trust, then a Black consumer has reason to *test* Black salespeople, because there are a number of issues that can be called into question:

a. Can I trust them to know what they are talking about: If you study Black salespeople, they almost always seem to be *new* salespeople. The enthusiasm that they generate is often a sign of their naivete about the problems that surround their product and industry. Most new salespeople are so desperate for sales that they won't dare tell you about the drawbacks of their product, figuring that you might use just that excuse not to buy. Experienced, secure, objective salespeople are what our community needs.

b. Can I trust that this is the best price available: Black-owned and operated establishments labor under the problems of high costs and low volume. Rarely have similar businesses come together to do any collective buying although lip service has been given to this idea for decades. Black consumers, usually with limited funds, are right to be dollar conscious, but unfortunately, they always seem to be this way with the Black retailer. All the rest of the time they seem to believe in the "you get what you pay for" philosophy. Like anything else it's a matter of degree. A five or ten percent mark-up over a comparable item in a White store is not going to hurt anyone's basic lifestyle. But a twenty percent difference says that this store owner needs a talking to.

c. Can I trust the service after the sale: You hear more and more about the country becoming a service economy. Because the Asian nations are producing an increasing number of U.S. consumer products, virtually every retailer can offer cheaper prices on many items. The question is who repairs, exchanges or at least listens later on down the line if there are problems. Black businesses, even in the best of times and conditions (and we don't know when that was really) were never known for refunds, exchanges, repairs or any other freebies. It is time that Black businesses start a new chapter which addresses the service aspect of business since it is fast becoming a part of this country's economic future.

d. Can I generally trust them to do what they say they are going to do?: Black people may just be getting into a variety of sales positions today, but previously our community had craftsmen to deal with. Craftsmen were like traveling salesmen. You didn't go to their stores, they came to your door and sold a few hundred or a few thousand dollars worth of plumbing, carpentry, roofing, masonry work, or other products and services. The stories about the dependability of (or the lack thereof) those Black tradesmen could fill up the Library of Congress, and those that weren't tragic would be hysterically funny to everyone except the victims. It is on this unfortunate foundation that we build our expectations and assumptions about new Black salespeople. Will they deliver? The community has every reason to be skeptical. It is called experience, not necessarily self-hatred.

Building the Trust Factor

Black people must understand that they are just entering the selling game, and that other races and groups have been doing it in this country for decades, perhaps a century. Furthermore, these groups work together and, as of this year at least, we have not learned how to do that very well. To a certain extent, when Black people start working together in business, sales and economic development it will be a *double* turning point. It will be a time when the Black community begins to take more pride in Black businesses because there will be more of a collective effort. And, it will be also a time when non-Black businesspeople begin to trust us as they see that we trust each other enough to work together. Who can trust working with a people who can't work amongst themselves and who, more than any other group, *needs* to learn to work together? Who can trust the competence or intentions of a people who have downtown contacts (mayors, police, fire fighters, education and union leaders) college degrees, more than ample religious influence and still *refuse* to work together for economic development?

The overall reputation of Black salespeople as a group will be tied to their individual competence and success, their public relations efforts (in the media generation, P.R. is everything), as well as the reputation of the Black community itself in gaining some degree of economic sophistication and cooperation. That to me seems to be the very broad picture. For individual salespeople who cannot afford to wait for the actions of the masses, they must really learn how to bend over backwards to please the entire spectrum of customers and plan for the long haul. The following tips should help:

1. If you are looking for the deepest experience in learning how to deal with conservative, doubting White folks, join a Fortune 500 corporation. If you are weak and unprepared you will either be rejected, kicked out soon after you enter or stay there forever. If you go in with *a plan*, you will learn the basics, a few details and then *leave*, ready to start up your own thing. If prospects are going to mistrust you, it will be harder for them to do if you are wearing IBM stripes, Xerox stripes or those of a similar company.

2. Ask a lot of questions. People distrust people who do all the talking, don't give others a chance to speak and don't listen very well. It is hard for a customer to distrust you if you allow him/her to do the talking, especially if you are agreeing with much of what he/she is saying.

3. Use testimonial letters. Show that others have been not only pleased with your service, but also feel strongly enough to write a letter about it. Keep your confidence, but be humble enough to realize that you must constantly prove yourself, probably forever if you intend to grow.

4. Establish yourself before you meet prospects. Have you ever heard about a person several times before you actually met them and

then when you finally did meet, you said to yourself, "So this is so and so." At the point of meeting you have interest, curiosity and probably more than the average amount of belief in that person. As a Black salesperson perhaps you first need to get to your prospects once or twice by mail or phone so that when they do meet you they are more willing to let you influence them.

5. In the Black community, trust will be partially the result of a wait and see period. The overwhelming majority of Black businesses close relatively soon after opening. There is often a period of struggle, juggling resources and desperation before the final closing. Often this period lasts for a year or more. The Black community seldom gets a chance to see a *new*, stable Black business (old barbershops, restaurants, etc., seem to hold on) so one can understand their skepticism. Consistency over time will generate trust.

6. Community participation will win a significant degree of trust from Black consumers. There is a popular slogan, "giving back to the community", and often the community expects it from you whether you are operating at a profit or not. Intentions are important. If there is the obvious intention on the part of a Black salesperson or business to make a financial or other type of contribution to a local cause or youth program, it can translate into increased patronage.

7. Make it easier to buy. Part of the function of a Black business should be to enable its customers to obtain things that they may not qualify for at more established enterprises with stricter credit qualifications. This will involve more extensive financing programs, probably with higher interest rates. But when people learn that they can obtain something they want that they can't get at other places, they are usually willing to pay a reasonably higher price. If you make it easier for your customers to buy what they want from you, suspicion often falls by the wayside and you get the storm of traffic that you seek.

8. White employees and White fronts. The word "front" has always had a negative connotation when applied to business situa-

tions. The purpose of fronts is to deceive the buying public (or creditors for that matter) into thinking that an operation is owned by one person or group of people when, in fact, it is owned by another. Usually you hear about Black folks fronting bars, convenience stores and other small establishments for White owners. There is nothing illegal about fronts. In fact, if you were to look into the ownership of major corporations and real estate holdings in this country you would discover that what you think is American is, in fact, owned by Japanese, German, British, French or other non-American interests. Since Black Americans generate distrust in certain industries and enterprises, we ought to be wise enough and clever enough to hire White Americans to serve our best financial interests. That may rob some of the ego satisfaction of having a "Black" business, but satisfactory profits can do wonders for a wounded ego. Utilizing "the right individuals" to further one's business interests is just a good management decision. It will *cost* some Black businesses more to survive than some others, but in the end, as they say, it should all come out in the wash.

After The Sale Service

At some point in time, you have interacted with someone to the point where you felt that a new friendship had developed. Weeks or months later you run into this friend and either you do not recognize him/her or he/she does not recognize you. Or you see two people you know very well, and just as you start to introduce them you forget one of their names. It can be a rather embarrassing situation, but usually it is rather harmless if you have considerate friends. As a salesperson, however, you cannot afford to have people not recognize you or forget your name. Why? Because good salespeople develop good incomes through repeat business; and it is harder to get repeat business if people do not recognize you or remember your name. In order to prevent this from happening, you want to be sure to provide excellent after-the-sale service. I mentioned mailing lists, telephone calls and, under the right circumstances, drop-in visits as methods of servicing your clients. As a Black salesperson you may need repeat business more than the average salesperson, because your total range of real prospects may be more limited. Unfortunately, as a Black salesperson you may be easier to forget. If you serve a mostly White clientele it is certainly much easier for them, if you are outside of your sales environment, to not recognize your face even after you speak to them. Black customers may frequently recognize you, but they do not associate you with a place of business since most of their contacts are social ones. Actually you want to offer after-the-sale service for three reasons. First, you want to do it because it's a good business practice, period. Secondly, you want to do it because you want to be remembered. And thirdly, you want to do it because you know that it will not be expected of you.

People expect Blacks to take the money and run. We are not expected to follow through or follow-up. When you do the exact opposite of what someone expects, whether it is good or bad, they remember it. If you saw a chubby Jewish kid dunk on Michael Jordan or outrun Carl Lewis, would you remember that? Forever! When you give Black customers after-the-sale service you are giving them something that they are not used to, in many instances, and something they don't expect. You also give them hope that it *does* pay to support Black businesses and Black salespeople. On the other hand, failure to provide such service would convince some that "it doesn't make any difference who you give your money to, they all are going to forget you." One of the most fundamental goals of Black salespeople should be to kill the belief. If they don't, much of what has been stated here is of no value.

A Final Note On Role Playing

It is quite possible to find two people doing what appears to be exactly the same thing. However, on closer examination, when you look more closely at the intentions, motivations and strategies of the two individuals, you can often find that they are really doing two vastly different things, even though the visible actions are strikingly similar.

For example, you are riding in a car, you turn onto a street, and you see two men running toward you. One of the men is in a sweatsuit, perspiring and out of breath. The other man is in street clothes, not perspiring, but looks more tense, and is also out of breath. With the exception of the street clothes, the two men look like they are doing the same thing. On closer inspection, however, you see a big difference. The man in the sweatsuit is followed by a young teenage boy. Their intent was to go out for a peaceful, refreshing jog. When they return home they will shower, change clothes and feel exhilarated and energetic for the rest of the day. Their run is an entirely positive experience for them. The other man, however, is being chased by a pit bull terrier that is growling and barking. This runner is terrified because he is thinking of all the deaths that have been attributed to this animal in the last couple of years. When he escapes this pursuing animal he will be exhausted, angry, tense, embarrassed. He will go home, shower and try to forget the frightening incident. Running for him, on this day, will be an entirely negative experience. Again note, similar physical actions but very different motivations, intentions and results. Why do I bring it up? A few pages back I made reference to Black people playing roles, being phony, not knowing or liking themselves, and that the entire activity is caused by a poor self-image. I also stated that, even though their self-deceit is covered up by being in an environment full of phonies, many feel even worse over time when they admit to themselves that they have phony actions, airs and habits. I still stand by this assessment. However, there are many other Black people capable of playing similar roles, but because they have different intentions, motivations, and strategies they come out with vastly different results.

As Black people, we need to develop our *bi-cultural lives*. We need to understand our Africanness and know what it means in the entire course of historical world events and American history. On the other hand, we need to understand the values, strengths and weaknesses of the

European-American personality. And just as immigrants speak two languages, we too have the responsibility of learning two languages. One language, African-American or "Black English", should be seen as a validation, at least in part, of the Black American experience. Standard English should be spoken in a way that comforts the total spectrum of our business associates, because, from the 1980's on, it is about results not style. What I am suggesting is that there is nothing wrong with playing a role if you know what you are doing.

The Japanese and other Asian people play a role when they visit the U.S. So do the various billionaires from the Middle East. People all over the world adapt themselves to the cultures in power without much loss of personal identity because *they know who they are* and they *know their ultimate purposes*.

When Black Americans play roles there can easily be confusion and danger. We as a people are not crystal clear about who or what we are. We are ignorant of our African roots and its relationship to world development. So we do not actively claim it. Our true purpose is constantly confused as we continue to identify our best interests with a people and a nation that often doesn't see *our* best interests as *theirs*. And our racial agenda is reactionary with little strategic planning on the part of our national organizations, or so it seems. Our ultimate goals seem to be the most consistently debated topic; so obviously our actions are at best a hit and miss affair. Yet and still it is important that the most stable among us learn to play the roles with dignity and direction.

If being a successful Black salesperson is one of your aims, and if getting some of the White community's money into the Black community is another, then clearly role-playing will be necessary. Trust was the most often repeated word I noted in my research on sales. In order for White folks to do business with you, they must trust you. During this period in the evolution of Black American history, you will not be allowed to be your "natural" self. You must act out another personality for Whites to feel comfortable around you and to trust you. It is part of the compromise you must make. The important thing to remember is that the role is only harmful if you forget who you really are. In a sense, all present-day Black salespeople have to have a Bryant Gumbel routine that they can turn on on short notice. Our *ultimate purpose* is to make sure that our winnings will make this marketing-acting game all worthwhile.

SETTING GOALS
AND IMPROVING

On the preceding pages, I provided many hints and suggestions about how and why one should get involved in selling. These hints are like bricks lying on the ground. They are real, they are numerous, but they are relatively unimportant unless and until someone uses muscle and talent to lift, stack and organize the bricks into the wall, the house or the factory they have the potential to become. This information, like bricks on the ground, is real but of little use if one does not take the information, internalize it, and use it to develop him/herself into what he/she can potentially be. Developing a motivational system was mentioned earlier, but this chapter will expand on some of those points.

I believe that people have to respect their own lives like they do their cars. You control your car. You give it energy to move (fuel), you start it, drive it, maneuver it and stop it when and where you want. I know many people who need to do the same with their lives. They need to get some energy and drive themselves where they want to go (or at least where they now *think* they want to go) and maneuver through life as they would down a busy street. What does it take for a person to do this? In my opinion, it takes faith, values and goals. By faith I do not mean religious beliefs, although they are important. By faith I mean the belief that if given the right information, the right perspective, and a reasonable understanding of what to expect and how to deal with occurrences when they happen, there is a chance you might get to where you want to go. As a Black person, there are many historical reasons for your having little faith, very legitimate reasons. But opportunity is knocking hard today and you can make your own opportunity where none may seem to exist. Today's Black folks have more possibilities for their lives than any generation of Blacks in the history of our existence in America. Many people gave all they had so that *you* could be where you are now. If you blow it, you will waste not only your own life, but also the efforts of millions who came before you, and you will certainly be making it more difficult for those who come after you.

I don't spend an awful lot of time trying to raise people from the dead because I realized an important principle a few years ago. If you look at either history or current events you will note that "winning" people *choose themselves* for success. Much of life, Black life in particular, is based on *waiting to be selected.* In school we stand in lines, raise our hands and wait our turns to be selected for something we value. We apply to colleges, graduate schools, jobs, and for promotions, and wait for someone else to select *us* and decide *for us* whether or not we are going to fulfill *our dreams.* That is the fate of the common person.

Leaders start off by leading themselves first. They respect what others say and think of them (sometimes) but it doesn't have a whole lot to do with where they are going with their lives. Some people have always had faith in their own vision for a whole host of reasons and others may never have it.

After faith, people need values and goals that are not in conflict. Most motivational books talk about goals but few mention values. If you are an adult around thirty or so, you probably have values that are much older than your latest goals. If you seem to be getting no closer to your goals now than you were when you first set them, your problem could be that you have set goals that are in conflict with your true beliefs. Your true beliefs are so deep that they are part of your fundamental value system. This system is anchored and rooted in your brain, your habits, your speech, your environment and your very essence. If given the choice between your twenty day old goal and your twenty-two year old values, which do you think your conscious and unconscious mind will lean towards? You got it! Black folks *as a people* have values that work against them taking charge of their lives. They are rooted in our historical relationship with power and how we respond to it (rather than seize it). They are rooted in our religious beliefs. They are rooted in our leadership role models. If you want to be successful as a Black person in America, you will have to change some of your beliefs and values to the extent that they may conflict with some of the failure-prone beliefs of virtually everyone you love. Hell, just by deciding to go into sales you have broken with most of Black tradition. I am not going to tell you what to believe or exactly how you should shape your values. But I do ask you to really check yourself out and ask yourself what do you really believe and *what proof do you have that you believe it.* (Prove to yourself, not anyone else). If in doing some internal examination you are rethinking some of your values, beliefs and habits, then you are doing the preparatory work on which to build goals.

Multiple Goal Setting

One of the major purposes of setting goals is to excite and motivate the goal setter to discipline him/herself to work towards achieving them. But too often people who set goals fail to realize that point because the only goal they set is the "jackpot goal." The "jackpot goal" is that final goal that one is reaching for when all the dreams, contacts and efforts come together to boost one to their life's peak achievement. A lifetime goal might be: becoming mayor of your hometown, becoming a famous singer, accepting the Academy Award for best actor, or winning the middleweight boxing championship. Too often people identify their ultimate goals but do nothing about setting short-term or intermediate goals. As a result, their jackpot goal loses its excitement because it is very difficult to measure progress towards or celebrate achievements on the way to that goal since it was not articulated as a meaningful goal in the first place. The best way to maintain discipline is to *reward* discipline. The best way to reward discipline is to celebrate the achievement of a worthwhile objective that puts one squarely on target and on time to reach the jackpot goal. It must be remembered that the most important thing about a goal is the maintenance of discipline and sustained effort. It is only through effort (and a little luck) that you get nearer to any goal. So anything that can help prolong the desire to put forth the effort is a worthwhile goal. A goal is a means to other goals, as well as an end in itself.

Goals then should probably fall into these categories:
   a. The Jackpot Goal - maybe ten or more years away
   b. Medium Range Goals - about two to five years
   c. Yearly Goals
   d. Monthly or Seasonal Goals
   e. Weekly Agenda
   f. Daily agenda or things-to-do list

The average person would never carve up his/her life into the many categories and commitments listed above. But if you were to look at the training schedule of an Olympic-caliber athlete, or the series of drawings that an architect might prepare for a major, three-year project, you would see a set of sequential steps or goals in the planning. There is a great temptation to want to be an achiever in a country where all kinds of achievers get attention, money and special perks. On the other hand, there is a great temptation to be an ordinary person, live an ordinary life with no more than an ordinary amount of stress and problems. One of the major factors involved in being an achiever, regardless of whether it is in sales or anything else, is the individual's willingness to follow a preconceived plan, a well-thought-out series of goals. By a series of goals I mean that there is more than one set of goals. In order to be an achiever, one has to be concerned with not just the general or basic aspects of an undertaking, but also the *details*, the specialized areas within the overall undertaking. You know in selling, for instance, that prospecting, qualifying, presenting and handling objections are all special areas within the overall selling process. So when I talk about a *series* of goals, I mean that a person interested in achievement must develop goals within specialized areas in order to produce better, overall results. Some of these types of Goals may be as follows:

Skill Goals:
   a.   Learn to speak with notes
   b.   Learn to run the computer in an office
   c.   Learn to speak without a lisp
   d.   Learn to better color coordinate clothes

Activity Goals:

    After you become reasonably skilled in a particular area of selling, you may want to set *quantity goals* as a part of your development.

1. How many prospects identified in a single hour, day and week
2. How many presentations made in a day and/or week
3. How many referrals obtained this week, this month.

Although money is a primary motivator to salespeople, it often helps to take your mind off money periodically and concentrate on the activity that brings the money. Activity goals are important because, first, they help you master the activity; the theory being the more you do something, the better and more confident you become at doing it. Quantity makes for quality. The second reason why activity goals are important is because by doing the activity more times, results, sales and money should follow as a natural consequence. Finally, activity goals are good to demonstrate to yourself just how much you are capable of accomplishing in a day or week. It helps to raise your daily expectation of yourself when you know what your highest accomplishment is. For example, suppose I make three presentations of my product in a day, and it seems to take up my whole day. I then believe that my normal day should consist of between two or three presentations. Then along comes this idea of making, as a personal goal, a greater number of presentations in a normal work day. The "contest" period lasts a week, and on one particular day I make six presentations. Well, after having done it, I now know that I should raise my number of daily presentations to four, never make less than three, and expect to make five occasionally. As a consequence of talking to more people, and as a result of meeting new activity goals, I should make more money even if I do not increase the *percentage* of people I successfully close.

Efficiency Goals:

    Sometimes quantity leads to quality and sometimes quantity leads to carelessness. Therefore, you may want to set goals that relate specifically to quality. You could call them efficiency goals.

For example, a survey of the records say that during your probationary training period you actually sold a product of some kind to thirty percent of the people you presented to. Now you are more confident and knowledgeable about your product and the competition. You also feel better about the product itself. You may want to see the same number of people but increase your sales percentage by twenty points. Rather than selling to one-third of the people you talk to, you want to sell to half. After working hard just on percentage of sales, you might hit that mark in six months, making more money as a result. Suppose at *that* point you decide to see more people and work on *quantity*. Even if you fall back from a fifty percent sales mark to forty percent, if you see fifty percent more people, look how much more income that would mean for you.

Peak Performance Week:

In athletics, all teams look towards the playoffs and the championship. It is during that time that athletes, coaches and staff seek peak performance in all aspects of the sport. A conditioning peak, a confidence peak (you've heard the expression that team X is "on a roll"), and an intellectual peak, are all sought so that a team can "pull it all together" when they need to most. Very few people, relatively speaking, ever experience winning a significant championship. But many more people fortunately do experience what it is like to be their personal best. Defeat is easier to take when you know you were at your best, rather than wondering "what if" I had trained harder, studied the plays better, took off five more pounds, etc. In sales, many companies stage a contest very similar to a sports competition. There are points to be scored, bonuses, gifts and prizes to be won, promotion and publicity to be generated, etc. It is good for a salesperson to go through these peak weeks or sales contests, not necessarily because of the prospect of winning (though that is not to be discounted) but just so the person can experience what it is like to call on his/her total resources through an extended period of time. The "peaking" experience has several practical uses. First of all, it tells you where you rank in the order of things as compared to peers, competitors, your own standards, etc. You know if you are good, average or poor when you've participated in an all out effort, and you should want to know that. Secondly, it sets a level of performance which you can now *plan to surpass* at a future date. This is what people mean when they say competing against yourself. They mean competing against a standard that you set in an earlier state of development which you feel you can now surpass. This is very important because by making this standard the new goal to surpass, people get motivated and discipline themselves. They *believe* so strongly that they can do better, they move closer to their ultimate, or as I call it, their jackpot goal. The third reason that participating in any competitive effort is good is because it raises the level of what you expect from yourself on a daily basis. Noone is in peak form all the time. But when people know what they have done can do and are capable of doing, their personal pride usually requires that they perform at a minimum standard level all the time. In other words, the better people perform during periodic tests, the more likely it is that they will improve on a daily basis; they will increasingly expect more of themselves, and we have seen how expectation can affect final outcome.

The final value of using goals, standards and records is in maintaining interest levels. All games can become boring if noone is keeping score. Activity means little if one can't see it within some type of framework or pattern. To keep records and statistics on one's efforts is to open the door to the possibility that on any day that record can be surpassed. Sometimes people set records by accident or at least with no predetermined intention. Outstanding performances should be noted since they don't happen often enough for most people. If enthusiasm has been repeatedly cited as the single, most significant factor that gets people to purchase, then surely salespeople must have some source from which to draw enthusiasm themselves. Goals, records, standards, challenges, contests, awards and rewards are and should remain a part of selling.

Beyond the Fundamentals

In almost any undertaking, the teacher, mentor, coach or supervisor will always say stick to the fundamentals, master the fundamentals. I have made an effort to include the fundamentals of the selling game in this volume. But mere observation shows that high achievers go beyond the fundamentals in mastering their art, craft, sport or vocation. What are the "secrets of success" in the sales world? What is the difference in attitude, style or mechanics that causes one person to achieve mediocrity while another, of no greater talent, achieves excellence beyond expectation. It is not enough to merely say hard work, luck or timing. Offered here are some tips, picked up through research, personal experience, conversation, imagination and other means, which you can add to your current sales skills that may make a difference in your career. I make no claim that they are "secrets of success" because I know and you know that what works for one person may not work for another. Since one must make distinctions in product lines, income levels and the nature of markets serviced, almost nothing can be said without qualification. Nevertheless, I feel these hints can be integrated into many people's current patterns and styles. Most achievers:

a. *Diversify:* Many salespeople are successful because not all of their income is dependent on their selling skills. Since selling is a seasonal, feast or famine situation, many salespeople make the decision early on to reinvest some of their income in enterprises that bring in a more regular flow of money. This allows for not only a more regular payment of bills, but also a psychological advantage in their sales careers. Salespeople are supposed to be enthusiastic. But how can one be enthusiastic if he/she is depressed (which can usually be detected through body language, tone of voice or other means) because sales have fallen off, interest rates have risen, personal commissions are down and personal debts are very high. A diversified salesperson, who knows that income is coming from other sources to keep the family afloat, has a better chance of "putting up a good front" than the salesperson who relies solely on commissions. A diversified salesperson will not second guess sales as career as another non-diversified salesperson might. In short, a diversified salesperson stands a better chance of riding out the low points in sales, both financially and emotionally, and will probably produce better *during* the low point because of his/her diversification of income.

   b. *Study their successes as well as their failures:* Thinking can be hard work for alot of people and they don't do hard work unless they have to. When most people are attempting to learn a new skill or idea, they study it *until* they "catch on." After they catch on they just repeat their efforts without "thinking" about it. But achievers often study their undertakings all the time. They study how to do it, they study their weaknesses, and when they succeed they study *their successes*. In the Black community, we have an expression that says leave well enough alone. There is some merit to that idea. But if you don't believe your success is pure luck, if you believe it is happening because you are making it happen, doesn't it make sense to study yourself to learn *exactly* how and why you are making it happen so you can *keep on* making it happen? I think so, maybe you do to.

   c. *Learn to appreciate the tough ones:* I don't think in the normal course of events that people like problems, hassles, confusion and the like. Most people have quite enough stress in their lives, even under normal conditions, and they can always appreciate smooth operations. But one difference between an achiever and other folks is that when there is a problem he/she jumps into it with both feet rather than looking for a way to duck it. Part of the reason could be just an oversized ego looking to put another metal on the chest. But another part could be that one learns more from the tough situations than from the easy ones. When you win in a tough, problem-filled situation, it is just like reaching a goal. It gives you a better idea of who you are and what you can do. It alters, in your mind, your perception of what a real difficult problem is when you have solved a difficult problem already. Does this mean that achievers look for problems? Usually not. But they learn to de-mystify problems. They learn to break problems down into elemental parts, and, once these parts are identified, it becomes a rather routine situation. Achievers are sometimes called brilliant, and many times they are. Other times they are just people who refuse to be too scared to tackle the tough ones. Having guts is often mistaken for being brilliant. In a world where both are in rather short supply, I guess they are rather easy to confuse.

d. *Rebound well:* Achievers experience failure like the rest of us. As a matter of fact, I have read in several places, and I believe it myself, that achievers fail alot more than average people because they attempt to do much more than average people. The difference is that achievers emotionally rebound faster than other people. They can have an absolute disaster one week and by the next Monday morning you'd think they had won the lottery over the weekend. Part of it is a front, part is eternal optimism and faith, and part is a big ego and leftover confidence from previous successes. Achievers are like boxers and football players, who don't show that they are in awful pain. Perhaps it is possible to be so centered on one objective that you don't feel the pain. If a person can fool or convince him/herself (either way it doesn't make much difference), then he/she will probably be pretty successful in psyching everyone else out as well. One reason you can't let selling failures get you down too much is because, as many agree, the selling game doesn't work by logic. What do you expect? If people don't *buy* based on logic, how could selling be based on it.

e. *Don't confuse trying harder, persistence and pressuring:* It is very important for the novice to understand the difference between pressuring in sales and being persistent in sales. They seem very much alike, but they are different enough to make a difference. When a new sales recruit is not having much success at selling and he/she is told in a subtle way to *try harder*, he/she often goes out and either begs people to buy or pressures them to buy. Noone likes to be pressured. Few people respect a beggar and hardly anyone buys from someone they don't respect. Selling better is not selling something to someone without regard for whether they need it, can afford it or want it. A good salesperson has to be a good advisor. Trying harder for the sale means giving the prospect more information, comparisons, purchasing options, etc., to consider so that a better decision can be made. Trying harder is being more informative and more advisory in your manner. Being persistent means giving continuous advice and making continuous efforts to close. Being persistent also means digging deeper to get more information from the prospect. What is the underlying problem that the prospect is hesitant to reveal? What are the financial constraints that he/she must operate within? Working harder means taking the time and effort to put yourself in the client's shoes to see how you would address his/her situation if it were facing you.

Professional salespeople actively fight the image of the "high-pressure salesperson" because it's the very image that has made people reluctant to trust and fully utilize them.

At some point, however, people will simply call a persistent salesperson pushy or pressuring. At that point it may be a matter of opinion, but the customer is always right (right?). If you've done your job, you have given your prospects a lot to consider and think about. If you have done that, you can withdraw and approach them later. There is no real agreement as to where "pressure" falls on the selling spectrum, but there is general agreement on where professional selling skills stop and amateur tactics begin.

f. Hire other people to do the routine work: All beginning salespeople can afford to give complete, personalized attention to their customers. But as you become successful in sales, you become like all successful people: very busy. At some point you are going to have to hire people or services to do all the things you use to do yourself. This may include answering telephones, sending and reading mail, inquiring about credit information, keeping the mailing list of clients and prospects up to date, making travel arrangements, designing printed materials and dealing with the printer. Any person who is still doing all or most of these things him/herself has a long way to go before maximizing his/her effectiveness as a salesperson. He/she may be very busy, very happy, very well-liked, but not very effective. The choice is his/hers to make.

g. *Invest in self-improvement aids:* High achievers are not all alike in any way. Some of them are not even nice people, if you want me to be cold-blooded honest. Some high achievers are ego maniacs who believe they know everything, or they can't identify anyone they need to listen to. Fortunately, these people are in the minority as much as I can tell at this point. Many other high achievers in sales are quite willing to improve themselves and learn anything from anyone who has something to say. High on their list of personal purchases are all sorts of self-motivational audio and video tapes. Sales achievers, for the most part, are not featured in People magazine, on Sixty Minutes or the Johnny Carson show. The sales professional does not get as much encouragement to push on by the outside world as do professionals in other areas. I bet that you can name a half-dozen top anything (singers, doctors, lawyers, ministers, etc.) before you can name a half-dozen top salespeople. For that reason and others, salespeople often have to turn to themselves for stroking, motivation and information. Enter the sales teaching aids. Many salespeople spend hours listening to lectures and question and answer sessions, and watching demonstrations in order to widen their scope and vision. Selling, like music, has universal principles. A car salesman can learn something from a rug salesman and both can learn something from a lady that sells cosmetics or real estate. Many times people will watch or listen to a motivational instructional tape, not because they intend to copy the speaker, but because they are looking for their own idea bank to be triggered. In other words, many salespeople like to use their own creativity and use other people's presentations to draw out their own ideas. These types of achievers see: learning as fun, reading industry magazines and books as fun, and being around like-minded people as exciting. They see the need to invest in learning tools. Books, magazines and tapes are tools for the salesperson just as a wrench is a plumber's tool and a hammer is a carpenter's. Craftsmen have tool chests, sales pros have learning libraries. Is it absolutely necessary to instruct yourself with these motivational aids? Perhaps not, but the continuous relationship between these types of tapes and successful performance seems more than just coincidental.

Summary

In order for people to improve they must have faith, values and goals which are not in conflict. Black Americans, despite the many historical reasons for lacking faith, are in a better position to take advantage of opportunities today than any other generation of Black Americans. But in order to take advantage of these opportunities, some Blacks need to make a break from some of the values that are hindering them from pursuing their goals. Goals are very important because they excite and motivate achievers to discipline themselves to work toward their dreams. Goals should be of all kinds, including performance, activity, skill, efficiency and peak performance. In order to build the body, the will, and the intellect to peak points of efficiency, one should also set aside periods of time for "peak performance". During this time, a person would simply see how much he/she could accomplish say in a week's time. Such weeks would raise the level of expectation in many people and have a carry-over effect on the normal work weeks. In addition to the pursuit of goals, improving performance also involves adopting some concepts such as diversification of income, the study of one's personal success as well as failures, and viewing the really tough challenges as learning laboratories. Learning tools/aids are also crucial to success and there appears to be a definite relationship between people who use them and those who eventually become high achievers.

Very Serious Business Enterprises Distributor Opportunity

Very Serious Business Enterprises is a company with two primary goals:

1. To develop, distribute and sell books and materials specifically designed to educate Black Americans about business and/or economic advancement.

2. To distribute and sell materials (books, audio tapes, video tapes, etc.) developed by others which we feel will help Black Americans in their personal, professional, business or economic development.

In carrying our our purpose and goals we have gained at least three tangible rewards:

- We have seen specific economic gains by many of our readers
- We have made fair profits
- We have built excellent contacts and networks

> We have found that the best means of getting our products to the people they were designed for is through a network of individual distributors. Our distributors, like ourselves, have gained fair profits, interesting and supportive contacts and the satisfaction of helping people improve their financial circumstances.

Any person, business, organization or group can become a distributor of our material. By simply purchasing a minimum number of books (ten) a distributor is entitled to the wholesale rates. The discounts for our other products vary according to the specific products.

We welcome anyone who desires to join us in pushing for the development of more and better businesses for Black people.

PHOTOCOPY THIS PAGE (or type the appropriate information) and fill in the requested information below. Send it to:

VERY SERIOUS BUSINESS ENTERPRISES
P.O. Box 356
Newark, N.J. 07101
(609) 641-0776

☐ Add my name to your mailing list. I'd like a chance to examine any opportunity you wish to share with your readers. I am under no obligation to buy or sell anything.

☐ I'd like to order copies of these books. Enclosed is a check or money order for each copy I am requesting

☐ 1. GETTING BLACK FOLKS TO SELL $14.00

☐ 2. BLACK FOLKS GUIDE TO MAKING BIG MONEY IN AMERICA $12.95

☐ 3. BLACK FOLKS GUIDE TO BUSINESS SUCCESS $12.95

☐ 4. INTERNATIONAL BLACK BOOK REFERENCE GUIDE $12.00

☐ I'd like to sell your book in my shop, store, business or in a fund-raing project.

I understand that I must order *at least* ten books *in total* to get the wholesale rate.

GETTING BLACK FOLKS TO SELL $8.40 Wholesale
                                                $14.00 Retail

BLACK FOLKS GUIDE TO MAKING BIG MONEY IN AMERICA $7.75 Wholesale
                                                $12.95 Retail

BLACK FOLKS GUIDE TO BUSINESS SUCCESS $7.75 Wholesale
                                                $12.95 Retail

Name _____

Address _____

City _____ State _____ Zip _____

Telephone _____ Occupation _____

Major Business Interest _____